CFA INSTITUTE MEMBERS

to receive free printed copies . . .

of Research Foundation monographs, CFA Institute members may sign up for e-mail notifications.* We'll send you an e-mail when a new monograph is about to be published and provide you with the option of receiving it in print for free. Simply e-mail us at **rf@cfainstitute.org** to let us know that you'd like to be included in these e-mail notifications.

Please note that all monographs are available for free online at www.cfapubs.org for both members and nonmembers.

*This service is available only to CFA Institute members.

For more on the Research Foundation of CFA Institute, please visit www.cfainstitute.org/research/index.html.

RESEARCH FOUNDATION CONTRIBUTION FORM

☑ **Yes,** I want the Research Foundation to continue to fund innovative research that advances the investment management profession. Please accept my tax-deductible contribution at the following level:

- ☐ Contributing Research Fellow ....$25,000 to $49,999
- ☐ Research Fellow ....$10,000 to $24,999
- ☐ Contributing Donor ....$1,000 to $9,999
- ☐ Donor ....$100 to $999
- ☐ Friend ....$ _____

☐ My check is enclosed (payable to the Research Foundation of CFA Institute).
☐ I would like to donate appreciated securities (send me information).
☐ Please charge my donation of $ _____ to my credit card.
   ☐ VISA ☐ MC ☐ Amex ☐ Diners ☐ Corporate ☐ Personal

Card Number

____/____
Expiration Date   Name on card PLEASE PRINT
☐ Corporate Card
☐ Personal Card
                         Signature

☐ This is a pledge. Please bill me for my donation of $ _____.

☐ I would like recognition of my donation to be:
   ☐ Individual donation ☐ Corporate donation ☐ Different individual

_____
PLEASE PRINT NAME OR COMPANY NAME AS YOU WOULD LIKE IT TO APPEAR

PLEASE PRINT ☐ Mr. ☐ Mrs. ☐ Ms.   MEMBER NUMBER _____

_____
Last Name (Family Name)   First   Middle Initial

_____
Title

_____
Address

_____
City   State/Province   Country ZIP/Postal Code

7OBR

**Please mail this completed form with your contribution to:
Research Foundation • P.O. Box 3668
Charlottesville, VA 22903-0668 USA**

For more on the Research Foundation of CFA Institute, please visit www.cfainstitute.org/research/index.html.

Thomas Oberlechner
Webster University Vienna

The Psychology of Ethics in the Finance and Investment Industry

Statement of Purpose

The Research Foundation of CFA Institute is a not-for-profit organization established to promote the development and dissemination of relevant research for investment practitioners worldwide.

Neither the Research Foundation, CFA Institute, nor the publication's editorial staff is responsible for facts and opinions presented in this publication. This publication reflects the views of the author(s) and does not represent the official views of the Research Foundation or CFA Institute.

The Research Foundation of CFA Institute and the Research Foundation logo are trademarks owned by The Research Foundation of CFA Institute. CFA®, Chartered Financial Analyst®, AIMR-PPS®, and GIPS® are just a few of the trademarks owned by CFA Institute. To view a list of CFA Institute trademarks and the Guide for the Use of CFA Institute Marks, please visit our website at www.cfainstitute.org.

©2007 The Research Foundation of CFA Institute

All rights reserved. No part of this publication may be reproduced, stored in a retrieval system, or transmitted, in any form or by any means, electronic, mechanical, photocopying, recording, or otherwise, without the prior written permission of the copyright holder.

This publication is designed to provide accurate and authoritative information in regard to the subject matter covered. It is sold with the understanding that the publisher is not engaged in rendering legal, accounting, or other professional service. If legal advice or other expert assistance is required, the services of a competent professional should be sought.

ISBN 978-0-943205-95-3

26 June 2007

Editorial Staff

Elizabeth A. Collins
Book Editor

David L. Hess
Assistant Editor

Kara H. Morris
Production Manager

Lois Carrier
Production Specialist

The Psychology of Ethics in the Finance and Investment Industry

Biography

Thomas Oberlechner is professor of psychology at Webster University in Vienna. His research on psychological aspects of decision making in financial markets has led him onto the trading floors of many of the world's leading markets; results have appeared in numerous academic and professional journals in psychology and finance. He is also the author of *The Psychology of the Foreign Exchange Market*. Professor Oberlechner has extensive experience as an instructor at executive seminars and professional development programs. He also deals with questions of ethics in his practice as a clinical psychologist and management coach. Professor Oberlechner holds an EdM in counseling and consulting psychology from Harvard University and a PhD and JD from the University of Vienna.

Acknowledgments

I want to thank the Research Foundation of CFA Institute for its interest in this fascinating topic and for its funding of this monograph. Also, I thank Mark P. Kritzman, CFA, for stimulating my interest in this subject and for our most enjoyable and insightful conversations about the links between psychology and finance. I am especially grateful to Raluca Roibu and Elisabeth Szumowski for their valuable research assistance and to Samia Geldner for her support in editing the manuscript. Institutional support for this research was provided by Webster University and Harvard University. Gerlinde Berghofer, Marshall Carter, Cornelia Eder, Ben Fasching-Gray, Carol Osler, and Viktor Mayer-Schoenberger provided me with helpful suggestions and support at various stages of the research and writing processes that led to this monograph. I am also grateful to Larry Siegel, research director of the Research Foundation, for support in this the project. Thank you all.

Contents

Foreword		vii
Preface: Toward a Psychology of Ethics in Finance and Investment		ix
Chapter 1.	Ethics in the Financial and Investment Industry	1
Chapter 2.	Defining Ethics and What Is Ethical	6
Chapter 3.	Psychological and Descriptive Understanding of Ethical Decision Making	14
Chapter 4.	Individual Ethical Development	21
Chapter 5.	Ethics-Related Individual Characteristics	26
Chapter 6.	Implicit Individual Processes	32
Chapter 7.	Social Influences on Ethics	39
Chapter 8.	Groups and Ethics	46
Chapter 9.	Power, Leadership, and Ethics	51
Chapter 10.	Organizational Culture and Ethics	56
Chapter 11.	Compensation and Reward Systems	61
Chapter 12.	Ethics Training	66
Chapter 13.	Conclusion	72
References		74

This publication qualifies for 5 PD credits under the guidelines of the CFA Institute Professional Development Program.

Foreword

Ethics is notoriously hard to write about. "Don't steal money" is just about the only rule that everyone in the investment profession would agree on. Beyond that, each person has his or her own point of view.

Why? One reason is that ethics is personal. The philosopher-businessman Nassim Nicholas Taleb has argued that there are some topics about which experts are much more knowledgeable than nonexperts (brain surgery, astrophysics, and car repair come to mind) and there are topics about which "experts" have little advantage over nonexperts.[1] Among the latter are religion, politics, and ethics. So, agreement on standards of ethical behavior is inherently difficult.

But ethical problems seem more vexing in the financial markets than in many other facets of life. In the markets, ethical concerns have come to the forefront because of the sheer size and economic impact of a seemingly endless parade of scandals. Why are financial markets peculiarly amenable to unethical behavior and attractive to unethical people?

A clue lies in the theory of the firm as set forth by Ronald Coase, the 1991 Nobel Laureate in Economics. Coase noted that all of the economic functions that are in fact performed by firms could, theoretically, be performed by individuals acting on their own behalf and transacting with each other at arm's length.[2] The problem with this "cowboy" design for the economy is that transaction costs would be crushing. So, society has organized itself into firms in which principals (shareholders) hire agents (managers) to coordinate economic effort, and transaction costs are thereby dramatically reduced.

This more efficient design creates a new cost, however, that arises from the *principal–agent conflict*. What is good for the manager is not necessarily good for the shareholder, and vice versa. Thus, if we are going to have an efficiently functioning economy in which firms are the source of most of the production, we are going to suffer some agency costs (the costs caused by agents acting in ways that are not in the best interests of the principals).

We had better manage these costs effectively. One way to do so is to enact wise laws and to enforce them diligently. Another way—the topic of the present volume— is to motivate agents to behave ethically, which, in this context, means something like "in the interest of the principals or as close to that as is possible in practice."

---

[1] See N.N. Taleb, *The Black Swan: The Impact of the Highly Improbable* (New York: Random House, 2007):146.
[2] R. Coase, "The Nature of the Firm," *Economica*, vol. 4, no. 16 (November 1937):386–405.

And in financial markets, motivating ethical behavior is both more difficult and economically more important than it is in activities that are more self-regulating. For example, compare an investment management firm with a hardware store. A hardware store owner has some incentive to cheat the store's customers (and a hardware store employee has some incentive to cheat his or her boss). The small service area covered by a hardware store, however, practically guarantees that a store that cheats its customers will earn a bad reputation and will lose business to competitors.

Moreover, in a hardware store, the stakes are too low to motivate any serious level of cheating. But in an investment management firm managing $1 trillion, an employee who can direct only one-millionth of those assets to himself to herself can become a millionaire. The temptation is great. And if the one-millionth is removed from all the clients' accounts evenly, none of them is likely to notice or be much harmed, which will soothe the conscience of the unethical trader. So, ethical behavior in financial markets will always be difficult to achieve.

It is in this context that Thomas Oberlechner applies concepts and findings from the field of psychology to develop a variety of methods for understanding, and teaching about, ethics in financial markets. To see why using psychology to understand financial ethics is almost imperative, let us momentarily force an ethical decision into the economist's standard model of a utility-maximizing individual.

To decide whether to commit an ethics violation, such an individual has to estimate the expected utility of the financial gain from the unethical behavior. But that estimate is just a start. He or she also has to estimate the cost, which includes (1) the expected disutility of being caught, where the likelihood of being caught is also a factor, and (2) the disutility of having a guilty conscience. These last components are obviously psychological, and Professor Oberlechner's deep knowledge of the body of research in psychology—which is unfamiliar to most readers with only a finance education—makes his discussion of the connection between psychology and financial market ethics lively and informative.

Professor Oberlechner presents his research and arguments with a light touch—a necessity when dealing with such a serious subject. He provides surprising insights on familiar stories from the news and makes useful connections between psychological research and financial market applications. We are delighted to present his work.

Laurence B. Siegel
Research Director
The Research Foundation of CFA Institute

Preface: Toward a Psychology of Ethics in Finance and Investment

Every day, we can read in the newspapers about violations of ethics and the law committed by professionals in the finance and investment industry. Similarly, almost every day, we can read statements by government officials and representatives of the financial industry about the danger of these violations to the reputation of the industry, appeals for better ethical behavior of the professionals active in this industry, and calls for stricter laws that, supposedly, will guarantee ethical conduct.

One of the organizations enforcing ethical standards is CFA Institute. With members in more than 130 countries around the world, its mission explicitly defines the following goal: "to lead the investment profession globally by setting the highest standards of ethics, education, and professional excellence" (CFA Institute 2007). A key to accomplishing this mission is the enforcement of ethical conduct of members through the Professional Conduct Program. Every CFA Program candidate and member of CFA Institute must annually sign and always abide by the Code of Ethics and Standards of Professional Conduct (CFA Institute 2005).

Laws and regulations are not enough, however, to maintain ethical standards in the behavior of investment professionals or to create a truly ethical culture in the industry. In addition, we need to direct our attention to psychology. Only if we learn about the psychological dynamics involved in ethical decision making will we understand why some finance and investment professionals behave highly ethically whereas others blatantly violate standards of ethical conduct and sometimes even break the law. Learning about the psychology of ethics will also give us the ability to manage ethical behavior more effectively. This ability applies to our own ethical conduct as well as to the conduct of others (Trevino and Nelson 2007)—that is, to the behavior of subordinates, colleagues, and supervisors. Moreover, understanding the psychology involved in ethics can form a basis for effectively influencing the organizations and the industry in which we work to promote fair and personally fulfilling professional environments.

Resolving Ethical Conflicts of Interest

Investment professionals manage other people's money. To maintain public trust in their activities, these professionals should live up to high standards of ethical behavior (Baker and Veit 1998). A basic tension exists at the very heart of the industry, however, that regularly places investment professionals in situations where they must decide whether to engage in ethical or unethical behavior. Often, behaving ethically means forgoing a short-term opportunity that would benefit either the professionals personally or their companies to the detriment of clients.

Thus, the role of investment professionals is inherently one of attempting to balance conflicting interests. Depending on their role in the company, practitioners may be beleaguered by the interests of their supervisors, the interests of their clients, and their own personal interests (Newsome 2005).

Investment professionals may find themselves in the ambivalent situation of being pushed toward two different ideals: profitability and ethical behavior, such as adherence to a professional or corporate code of conduct (Dobson 1997). This basic tension in which financial and investment professionals operate can make the concept of a "good" professional confusing. A first reaction might be to dismiss unethical practices as inevitable and systematically inherent in an industry whose main focus seems to be wealth maximization. Doing so means simply accepting the investment industry as a polluted environment full of negative and harmful side effects (Lamb 1999).

Is this conclusion the only option? On the one hand, because the investment industry by its nature involves conflicting ideals, it may never be possible to eliminate conflicts of interest through regulation (Jennings 2005; Newsome 2005). On the other hand, fortunately, a solution is possible that allows finance and investment professionals to rise above the perceived "either/or" nature involved in their conflict of interests. This remedy invites them to transcend the basic tension inherent to their profession through the psychology of ethics.

Psychology's Contributions to Ethics

The fundamental value psychology plays in resolving this conflict would be hard to overestimate:

- Psychology examines and describes how (un)ethical people actually behave.
- Psychology offers insights into the actual individual motives for (un)ethical behavior of people and the individual cognitive and emotional dynamics that underlie this behavior.
- Psychology creates an understanding of situation-specific and task-specific influences on the ethics of people's decisions and behavior.
- Moving beyond the immediate situation, psychology allows identification of ethics-nurturing versus ethically hostile organizations and environments.
- Psychology raises the awareness and the number of behavior alternatives available to people regarding their own ethical behavior.
- Psychology provides advice to managers and other professionals on how to support ethical behavior in others and how to implement changes in their organizations to foster ethical behavior.
- By contrasting self-actualizing professionals to the economic notion of rational individual actors maximizing their profits, psychology offers a set of (implicit) values and assumptions about what "good work" and "a fulfilling life" mean.

Thus, psychology takes center stage in the ethics of the finance and investment industry; it does not play a merely supporting role.

Defining what is ethical decision making in the investment industry is simple when the nature of the facts is obvious and the choice is black and white—that is, when we know one side to be clearly right and the other to be clearly wrong. In vague situations where different points of view seem possible and responsibilities and values conflict, ethics turns into a completely different enterprise. Such challenging situations may lead to painful inner conflicts and require finance and investment professionals to weigh and choose between deeply held values or between significant ideals (Andrews 1989; Badaracco 1998).

The following chapters provide practical insights into how professionals consider ethics in their daily decisions and into the psychological processes that determine how ethical the decisions are. We will explore how investment professionals sometimes make morally wrong decisions against their better judgment in situations that are crystal clear but also how they can act most ethically in the midst of conflicting values and despite the temptations and possible rewards for a choice that is less than ethical.

—T.O.

1. Ethics in the Financial and Investment Industry

In 1999, before the dot-com bubble burst, the second season of the television series "The Sopranos" went on the air. In this series, the family, unwilling to miss out on all that dot-com action, starts pushing the stock of an obscure technology company, Webistics, on unsuspecting retirees. They use brokers who know that the stock is a "dog" because of the company's outdated technology:

Broker 1 (talking on the phone with a customer): You know, from what you told me, Webistics would be perfect for your portfolio. I understand you're on a fixed income, but with Webistics, you could triple your money in a year. Uh-huh, yeah, 10, 12 months. I really shouldn't be telling you this. The company's Webistics. It's the next Yahoo! right now. We're really only selling it to preferred clients.

Broker 2 (on the phone with a customer): Yeah, American Forestry, 19 and 1/2, up 3/8s, a very sound company. Well, it depends on whether you wanna go for growth or value. We got hundreds of mutual funds you can choose from.

Broker 1 (while punching Broker 2): Ahh! You're supposed to push Webistics!

Broker 2: I was giving them alternatives.

Broker 1: Webistics is our pick of the week!

After the stock price has risen considerably, the family sells out its position in the stock and cashes in on the profits.

This story paints the nightmare scenario for any investor. The Sopranos are a fictitious TV family, but the question is whether something like this scenario could happen in reality. Apparently, it can. In June 2003, in San Diego, newspaper headlines announced the indictment of eight employees of the brokerage firm Hampton Porter Investment Bankers. These investment professionals had been involved in a securities fraud scheme that affected more than 100 investors throughout the United States, with registered losses of US$5 million.

Through their investment banking deals and from other sources, the investment bankers allegedly obtained and controlled a large number of shares of certain low-priced thinly traded "penny stocks." The brokers allegedly received special undisclosed incentive payments to push the sale of these stocks through a variety of high pressure, deceptive sales tactics. Once customers bought the stocks, raising their prices, the co-conspirators allegedly sold their shares and reaped huge profits. The indictment further alleges that the defendants prevented customers from selling their shares of the stocks by delaying or failing to execute the customers' sell orders (Department of Justice 2003).

This real-life story of what is often called a "pump and dump" ploy depicts one of the many schemes that was going on at the height of the dot-com boom. One of the traded shares involved in the fraud could very well have been a "Webistics."

Now, the bubble has burst, accounting and investment fraud scandals have gone public, large financial firms have collapsed, and top executives have gone to prison. Fraud schemes, however, such as the one portrayed on "The Sopranos" and implemented in real life by the Hampton Porter employees, are as prevalent today as they were in 1999, and they seem to be proliferating. Ethical scandals are too numerous to label as temporary aberrations or samples of abnormal behavior, and they range from petty to high-profile skullduggery.

Ethical Vulnerabilities of the Investment Professions

The periodic waves of ethical scandals in the finance and investment industry have been followed by severe scrutiny and legal reforms (Jennings 2005; Weirich and Rouse 2003). For example, in the bull market of the 1990s, many in-house analysts had strong incentives to bolster their banks' investment operations. These incentives corrupted the objectivity of their research and recommendations. As a result of the subsequent public protest, the settlement between state and federal securities regulators and 10 of the largest Wall Street firms imposed structural reforms and required disclosure of analysts' recommendations (see www.oag.state.ny.us/press/2002/dec/dec20b_02.html).

During these scandals, professionals in the fields of finance and investment did not manage their ethical image well in the eyes of the public. Gallup Polls conducted in the past decade on the perceived ethics of various occupations indicate that "bankers" are losing status and that "stockbrokers" have repeatedly been rated among the least ethical professions.

Moreover, in the new millennium, after the demise of Enron Corporation, WorldCom, and Arthur Andersen, the ethical standards of "business executives" have been rated by many as low or very low (Stevens 2004). Again, a heated debate about reforming and increasing regulation of the financial and investment industry and U.S. corporations resulted. In response, the Sarbanes–Oxley Act of 2002 introduced tighter regulations on corporate governance and financial disclosure (Newsome 2005).

Having shattered the trust of the public and having attracted the wrath of the regulators, the investment industry has been forced to question and redefine its ethical fundamentals. The fact is that a large number of factors inherent in the investment industry make this professional field vulnerable to ethical breakdown. To begin with, temptations to profit from unethical behavior are often larger in finance than in any other field. Although this conclusion seems obvious, it is also easily underrated, as the following anecdote warns. As the story goes, when Willie Sutton was asked why he robbed banks, he replied, "Because that's where the money is" (Bernstein 2006).

In addition, the professional barriers to entering the investment industry are limited. Therefore, the barriers may be crossed by people of a large variety of professional backgrounds. One result is that achieving a common ethical understanding is difficult (Caccese 1997).

A look at how scandals and complaints are handled in the medical field, in religious organizations, and in the military suggests that all professional environments tend to sanction and internally validate the actions of their practitioners—even when they are unethical. The self-justifying dynamics involved in this phenomenon may be particularly pertinent in the area of finance and investment (Bernstein 2006).

Moreover, in recent years, financial and investment activity has grown much more rapidly than the rest of the economy. This explosive growth has been accompanied by a great deal of specialization among finance professionals, who work in increasingly complex organizations. Increased specialization and complexity may dim financial actors' views of their actions' consequences in a significant way. For example, finance experts have noticed that technology has isolated their work from the "real economy" and that the institutions and the culture of the finance and investment sector are now often far away from other areas of the economy. In addition, many of the theoretical models and paradigms of finance do not encompass the social complexities of the economy, let alone of society. A case in point: The paradigm of perfect capital markets that governs many financial models suggests that individual players have no influence on the market.[3] This lack of influence distances the actors in finance and investment from the consequences of their actions and allows them to lose sight of their personal responsibility (Bonvin and Dembinski 2002).

All of these factors show that ethics in the investment profession is not only complex but also highly vulnerable. These factors correspond to psychological findings on the conditions that increase the likelihood of people committing harmful and unethical actions in everyday life. As a field study by noted psychologist Philip Zimbardo has shown, anonymous environments bring about unethical vandalism. In his study, Zimbardo placed abandoned cars with license plates removed and hoods raised in two highly different social environments, Palo Alto, California, and the Bronx, in New York City.[4] The cars were secretly filmed from some distance away. In the Bronx, it took no more than 10 minutes for the first vandals to begin their work of destruction, and within 2 days, more than 20 acts of

---

[3] A perfect capital market is one in which all participants are "price takers" and none are "price makers"; that is, no individual participant has any effect on market prices.

[4] Palo Alto is one of *Money* magazine's "Best Places to Live" (2006); the population is about 57,000 and median annual household income is about US$133,000. The Bronx has been considered an area in need of redevelopment. In the 2000 U.S. census, the Bronx had a population of 1.3 million and median annual household income of under $28,000.

theft or damage had been committed. All but one of these certainly unethical and often highly destructive acts were committed by adults, many of them well dressed and driving their own cars. In contrast, no single act of vandalism was recorded in Palo Alto over the duration of a work week. Instead, when the car was removed by the experimenters, three residents informed the police that a car was about to be stolen (Zimbardo 1976).

Zimbardo (2004) explained the differences in these two outcomes as follows:

> Any environmental or societal conditions that contribute to making some members of society feel that they are anonymous—that no one knows or cares who they are, that no one recognizes their individuality and thus their humanity—makes them potential assassins and vandals, a danger to my person and my property—and yours. (p. 33)

This explanation brings to mind the picture of global financial markets, where faceless players across the globe engage in transactions and where the traded commodity is no more than abstract numbers. Environmental anonymity is a condition of countless transactions in today's financial markets. Thus, the very nature of this professional field is certain to pose a formidable challenge to ethical behavior.

Why Are *Any* Investment Professionals Ethical?

Another challenge to ethics in the field of finance and investment is revealed by the question of why professionals in this field should be ethical at all. In many of today's curricula in the business schools that investment professionals proudly attend, the objective of rational individuals is wealth maximization. According to the dominant neoclassical economic perspective, ethics, in this context, functions as a behavioral constraint (Dobson 1993). This kind of thinking is reflected in, for example, codes of "ethics" and rules of compliance that aim purely at avoiding the costs that engaging in unethical behavior would entail for the company. It is also reflected in the focus of various industry watchdogs on protecting the unsophisticated consumer and maintaining standards and control systems throughout the industry. Finally, this understanding of ethics is reflected in investment organizations that define reputation, integrity, and being ethical not by their intrinsic worth but in materialistic terms, where these "values" represent no more than another means to the actual end of profit maximization.

Fortunately, the neoclassical economic view of self-interest is being increasingly challenged by psychological theories and findings. These findings suggest that people *want* to be ethical and have an intrinsic interest in being ethical that does not rest on extrinsic punishments or other outside factors (Vidaver-Cohen 2001).

Proponents of the economic view of human self-interest often cite Adam Smith, who famously declared, "It is not from the benevolence of the butcher, the brewer, or the baker that we expect our dinner but from their regard to their own interest" (Smith 1904). MacIntyre (1999) asked, however, if we enter the butcher's shop only to find him on the floor of the shop suffering a heart attack, is it probable that we would follow in a self-interested way the norms of the market, leave him dying on the floor, and simply finish our purchase at the butcher next door? No, in this situation, even the toughest finance pro would probably come to the aid of the butcher and call an ambulance (Bernstein 2006; Dobson 2005). Thus, the maxim that people are *only* self-interested is ideologically normative, not a description of real behavior (Miller 2001).

That ethical values and justice motivate the decisions of economic decision makers has also been demonstrated by psychologists in the "ultimatum game." This game is played by two players. The first player's task is to divide €10 between herself and the other player. For example, she could suggest that both players receive €5 or that she keep €8 and the other player receive €2. The division is an "ultimatum" because either the second player accepts and the division is made or the second player refuses and neither player receives anything. From the viewpoint of economic rationality and self-interest, the second player should thankfully accept even an offer of 1 cent because from a viewpoint of egoistic self-interest, 1 cent is better than nothing. Psychologists have shown, however, that offers far below €5 are usually rejected.[5] Such offers are perceived to be immoral; they violate basic values of justice and fairness. Thus, the ultimatum game shows that defending these ethical values is more important to players than profit maximization.

For a better understanding of ethics in the financial and investment industry, the question of what motivates people—in particular, financial and investment professionals—to be ethical is crucial. In the present day, fortunately, our knowledge about how to answer this question is greater than ever before (Dienhart, Moberg, and Duska 2001). To answer the question, we should remember that throughout the history of philosophy, ethics has been viewed as a motivation, not as a constraint (Dobson 1993), and this view is confirmed today by psychology.

---

[5] See Bethwaite and Tompkinson (1996); Güth, Kliemt, and Ockenfels (2003); Güth and Tietz (1990).

2. Defining Ethics and What Is Ethical

To many professionals, the topic of ethics seems to be something esoteric, far away from the reality of their work life and the situations they encounter day by day (Trevino and Nelson 2007). Thus, relevant questions in this monograph are the following: What does "ethics" actually mean? Why should ethical decision making in the finance and investment industry be looked at not only from an abstract, philosophical viewpoint but also from a psychological viewpoint? To answer these questions, this chapter defines ethics, lists the challenges to ethics inherent to the professional field of finance and investment, and explains the nature and limitations of three fundamentally different philosophical approaches in judging the ethics of investment professionals.

What Is Ethics?

Ethics can generally be understood as "rules of behavior based on beliefs about how things should be" (De Mott 2001). Abstract definitions of ethics range from "a set of moral principles or values" to "the principles, norms, and standards of conduct governing an individual or group" (Trevino and Nelson 2007, p. 13). The field of ethics in the investment industry thus is the study of situations and decisions in the industry that address moral issues of right and wrong.[6]

Determining whether something is right or wrong from an ethical viewpoint differs from analyzing it from a legal viewpoint. Although laws generally attempt to codify ethical considerations into specific rules and explicit regulations, ethics and the law are not the same (Crane and Matten 2004).[7] Many actions that are not explicitly prevented by the law may not be considered ethical (consider an investment bank executive allowing his girlfriend to use the corporate jet for personal travel). As Jennings (2005) noted, although finance professionals suffer from a dependency on laws and rules, they are myopic when it comes to ethics.

---

[6]Considerable variation in the usage of the terms "ethics" and "morality" exists (Kelemen and Peltonen 2001). This monograph uses the terms interchangeably.

[7]Laws may be unethical. For instance, an ordinance on "Registration of Jewish Assets" enacted in April 1938 in Germany under the National Socialists enabled the Commissary for the Four Year Plan, a state office, to take measures to ensure that the registered property was "deployed in accordance with the interests of the German economy" (James 2001, p. 5). James provides evidence that German financial institutions had at least a facilitating role under this and similar laws.

In fiscal year 2006 (ending 30 September 2006), the investor assistance staff at the U.S. Securities and Exchange Commission (SEC), the federal authority regulating the securities industry, received 20,663 complaints. The 10 most common complaints involved (1) advance-fee fraud, (2) unwanted e-mails or faxes, (3) manipulation of securities, prices, or markets, (4) transfer of accounts, (5) errors or omissions in account records, (6) problems with redemption, liquidation, or closing accounts, (7) delivery of funds or proceeds, (8) short selling, (9) difficulties in accessing accounts, and (10) problems with delivery of securities (SEC 2006).

These complaints indicate that many of the ethical issues in the investment industry involve questions that are addressed by such standards as the CFA Institute Code of Ethics and Standards of Professional Conduct (see CFA Institute 2005). For example, according to these standards, unethical behavior of financial analysts lies in making recommendations that are not based on diligence and thoroughness, composing research to support specified conclusions, leaking inside information, giving unfair preferential treatment to certain clients, plagiarizing, not telling the truth about a company's (expected) performance, front running (i.e., using new material information to trade for one's own accounts before trading for clients' accounts), and hiding from their employer or customer a conflict of interest (see Veit and Murphy 1996). Analysts may also use their insider knowledge for personal gain or incorrectly handle conflicts of interest between the "research" and the "underwriter" parts of investment companies (Jennings 2005). The insufficient management of these conflicts of interest is paid for dearly by customers and also by the investment public who trusts those analysts employed by investment banks: When markets perform poorly, independent investment analysis and advice are likely to be significantly better than the investment analysis and advice offered by in-house analysts who work for banks (Barber, Lehavy, McNichols, and Trueman 2006; Simon 2004).

Ethical issues in the investment industry arise not only between analyst and investor but also in various other relationships—between competitors, between employer and employee, between superior and subordinate, between adviser and client, and between an organization and its representative. Moreover, in addition to unethical practices that are specific to the finance and investment industry (Duska 2005), unethical behavior among professionals may include non-industry-specific behavior, such as the following: In a survey sent to several thousand workers in the United States, reported unethical actions arising from work pressure included such items as covered-up incidents, deceiving customers, putting inappropriate pressure on others, falsifying numbers, lying to superiors, withholding information, misusing company property, discriminating against coworkers, bribing, abusing expense accounts, leaking proprietary information, and accepting inappropriate gifts (Petry, Mujica, and Vickery 1998).

What is considered ethical misconduct in the investment industry may sometimes be an obvious and crystal clear violation of a value. Former SEC Chairman William Donaldson's summary of allegations against financial analyst Jack Grubman included the following:[8]

> [He] issued several fraudulent research reports that contained misstatements and omissions of material facts about the companies, contained recommendations contrary to his actual views regarding the companies, overlooked or minimized the risk of investing in these companies, and predicted substantial growth in the companies' revenues and earnings without a reasonable basis. The complaint against Grubman further alleges that he issued numerous research reports that were not based on principles of fair dealing and good faith, did not provide a sound basis for evaluating facts regarding the subject companies, and contained exaggerated or unwarranted claims about those companies. (Donaldson 2003)

As Jennings (2005) noted, "No one within the field looks at Jack Grubman . . ., the fee structures, the compensation systems, and the conflicts and frets, 'These were very nuanced ethical issues. I never would have seen those coming.'"

At other times, however, ethical dilemmas in the industry involve a true tension between important values—a conflict of "right versus right" (Kidder 1995, p. 13), a clash between contradictory duties (Newsome 2005). Imagine, for example, a young analyst deciding whether she should bypass the organizational line of command and report the seemingly questionable conduct of her immediate supervisor to top management. This analyst experiences tension between two goods: the welfare of the organization and her respect for her supervisor (see Fang 2006).

Much academic ink has beesn used to define ethics, and although all the abstract definitions shed valuable light on the nature of ethics, a definite and once-and-for-always valid definition of ethics is impossible. Such a definition may not even be necessary for the purposes of this monograph (i.e., to provide insights into the psychological dynamics involved in ethical and unethical behavior). Nevertheless, although all finance professionals have at least an implicit understanding of what ethics is about, it is important to stress that a genuine understanding of ethics in the finance and investment industry treats ethics as more than simply "avoiding wrongdoing."

Thus, ethics should be understood as not being limited to a set of prohibitive rules; it goes far beyond a mere catalog of do's and don'ts. The best understanding is to view the ethics of finance professionals as a value worth practicing as a goal in itself, a necessary condition of personal and professional excellence (Dobson 1997; Pritchard 1992). From this perspective, ethics in finance and investment is a driving force of a career that is well lived (Solomon 1999).

---

[8] Grubman was a highly paid telecommunications analyst at Salomon Smith Barney who championed Global Crossing and WorldCom (two clients of the firm's investment banking arm) even as the two companies plunged toward bankruptcy. The SEC, the New York Attorney General, and the New York Stock Exchange censured Grubman and permanently barred him from the securities industry in 2003.

Normative, Descriptive, and Prescriptive Approaches to Ethics

When people talk and write about ethics in the finance and investment industry, they approach the topic in a variety of ways and address different realms of ethics. Usually, their dealing with ethics takes one of three main directions: (1) what investment professionals should do, (2) what they actually do, or (3) how finance and investment professionals can be helped to get from what they actually do to what they should do.

1. *Normative ethics.* What should finance and investment professionals do? As the name implies, normative ethics aims at establishing norms and guidelines for professionals regarding how they should behave. This approach to ethics is inherent in, for example, the ethical theories of moral philosophy, theology, and definitions of professional norms, standards, and acceptable behavior for a professional field. Thus, a normative approach to ethics in finance and investments defines what is ethical in this profession. It tells practitioners how investment professionals should act to be ethical, which behavior should be considered ethical, and which behavior should not (Crane and Matten 2004). The guidelines and rules laid out in the CFA Institute Code of Ethics and Standards of Professional Conduct (CFA Institute 2005) address ethics in a normative way by establishing behavioral guidelines to which members must adhere.

2. *Descriptive ethics.* What do investment professionals actually do? Descriptive ethics aims at describing not how people should behave but how they actually do behave. And descriptive ethics attempts to explain and predict the (un)ethical behavior of people in real-life situations (O'Fallon and Butterfield 2005). Psychological research conducted in controlled laboratory studies and real-world settings of professional decision makers offers a systematic and comprehensive basis for descriptive ethics in finance and investing. Only this psychological and descriptive approach allows us to understand when and why people and organizations in the investment industry engage in ethical behavior and when and why they do not (Crane and Matten 2004).

3. *Prescriptive ethics.* How can finance and investment professionals be helped to get from what they actually do to what they should do? Based on descriptive insights about the factors influencing actual ethical decision making, the prescriptive approach to ethics aims at helping people and organizations toward ethical decision making by giving advice about how to create environments that foster ethical decisions and how to improve the ethical component of decisions. The two main questions addressed by prescriptive ethics are the following: How can we create organizations that foster ethical behavior? How can we train professionals to readily perceive the ethical dimensions of their own behavior and to act ethically? Thus, prescriptive ethics suggests tools that assist people in making the prescribed decisions (Trevino and Nelson 2007).

This overview of the normative, descriptive, and prescriptive approaches to ethics reveals that the aim of the present monograph is *not* normative in nature. Unlike the Code of Ethics and Standards of Professional Conduct, this monograph is not intended to tell investment professionals how they should decide and behave. The monograph is a descriptive summary of important insights into how investment professionals actually make decisions, and it reports research findings about the actual factors underlying (un)ethical decision making. Often, prescriptive conclusions and advice about how to improve the ethical dimension in decision making can be easily inferred from these descriptive insights; rarely will such advice be explicitly offered.

Normative Theories

However, as the saying goes, it is nice to know classical music before playing jazz. Thus, to provide a fuller understanding of the field of ethics in the finance and investment industry, this section provides a short (and necessarily superficial) overview of three of the most important *normative* theories in ethics—describing not how people actually make decisions but ideals of ethical decision making. These theories have been developed over centuries and constitute the major normative approaches to ethical decision making even today. The differences in what they define as ethics are largely based on where they place the focus in judging what is ethical—on the consequences of decisions, on universal duties and abstract principles, or on the personal character and virtue of the decision maker. The following overview also shows that when we face the complexities of situations and issues in the investment industry, no single approach guarantees perfect and simple solutions to ethical decision making (Trevino and Nelson 2007).

Judging Ethics by Consequences. To judge whether something is ethical, *consequentialist* theories strictly emphasize the consequences of the decision.[9] Of course, the consequences of actions matter in ethical decision making. In fact, economists and finance professionals are highly familiar with this approach to decision making. When they invest money, they look at the utility of financial decisions' outcomes and choose the course of action that results in the highest utility (e.g., the financial product or strategy that promises the highest risk-adjusted profit).

Only decision outcomes matter in consequentialist theories: The most ethical decision results in the greatest benefits (to society or to all stakeholders); an unethical decision results in disadvantages and harm (Trevino and Nelson 2007). The ethical utilitarianism reflected in consequentialist theories aims at maximizing

---

[9]Consequentialist theories are also called *teleological* theories, from the Greek word *telos*, which means end or goal.

the utility of a decision's outcome to society; an ethical decision simultaneously maximizes benefits and minimizes the harms to those affected by the decision.[10] Thus, these theories of ethical behavior are ends based (Kidder 1995).

Although the utilitarian approach is valuable in thinking about the ethics of a certain decision, efforts to base decisions exclusively on this approach quickly face practical limitations. Typically, decision makers do not have all the information necessary to foresee all consequences for everyone affected by a decision, and gathering this information may even be impossible. For example, Jeffrey Skilling, the president and chief executive officer of Enron Corporation, in effect, granted Chief Financial Officer Andrew Fastow a waiver from the conflict-of-interest rules in the company's code of ethics by allowing Fastow to establish a "special purpose entity" to reduce the company's fees at investment banks. At the time when Skilling agreed to this procedure, he may not have anticipated the destructive consequences of this conflict of interest but may have, instead, focused on the possible benefit of the reduced fees to Enron and the company's shareholders (Eichenwald 2005).

Another limitation of this approach is that consequentialist thinking can be used to justify evil by way of a calculated "greater good"—for example, when the continued sale of a dangerous product is known to result in a small number of predictable deaths, as in the case of the Ford Pinto. Despite media reports about incidents of Pintos burning after rear-end collisions and passengers dying from these fires, Ford Motor Company continued to produce and sell the car without modifications to the dangerous fuel tank that had been proven to easily rupture and catch fire. Ford knew that its path would lead to additional victims of fire after accidents but, based on a cost–benefit analysis, decided that the profit of the company outweighed the cost of anticipated casualties (Maclagan 1998). This example shows that using a strictly consequentialist approach can easily lead to a solution that sacrifices the interests of minorities and individuals in order to achieve the greatest good for the greatest number of people (Trevino and Nelson 2007).

Judging Ethics by Universal Duties and Principles. A second group of ethical theories focuses on universally valid duties and principles. These approaches emphasize the binding nature that abstract principles have on a decision regardless of the consequences of the decision. These philosophical approaches to ethics are labeled as *deontological*, which comes from the Greek word *deon* for duty or obligation. What is most important in deontological theories of ethics is adherence of the decision makers to principles—such as "keep your promises," "treat everybody fairly," and "always tell the truth" (Trevino and Nelson 2007). In other words, deontological ethics answers the question of how finance and investment

---

[10] Utilitarianism is commonly associated with the 19th century British economist and philosopher John Stuart Mill.

professionals should approach ethical issues by having them step out of the specific situation and use one or more universal principles to make the decision (Dobson 1997). Thus, these theories of ethical behavior are rule based (Kidder 1995).

Deontological thinking is primarily associated with the 18th century German philosopher Immanuel Kant's "categorical imperative." According to the categorical imperative, decision makers in a given situation should act according to the way in which they would like *everybody* to act in that situation. In Kant's words, "I ought never to act except in such a way that I can also will that my maxim should become a universal law" (Kidder 1995, p. 158). A well-known example of a deontological principle is the Golden Rule: "Do unto others as you would have them do unto you." Thus, finance professionals should ask themselves whether they would want the principle according to which they are acting to become a general standard, valid for everybody.

Difficulties when taking a deontological approach to decision making arise when two valid principles are opposed, as is the case in many ethical dilemmas. For example, the employees of an investment firm may find themselves caught in the dilemma between loyalty to their company's interests and truthfulness vis-à-vis their investment clientele. A purely deontological approach may not be able to solve the question of which side takes precedence over the other. Moreover, in many examples, deontological approaches to ethical decision making seriously conflict with consequentialist arguments, as in the example of the 1940s German homeowner who always tells the truth and informs the Gestapo about the Jewish family hiding in the attic (Trevino and Nelson 2007).

Judging Ethics by Personal Character and Virtue. Virtue ethics (or theories of virtue) emphasizes the character, motivation, and intention of the decision maker. The understanding of ethics in virtue ethics represents a comprehensive approach, not a specific approach, because it moves beyond the examination of single isolated issues or situations. It looks at ethics from an agent-based perspective, not an action-based perspective; it addresses characteristics of the decision maker's personality rather than particular actions (as in the rules and guidelines for actions in deontological theories) or consequences of actions (as in consequentialist theories) (Dobson 1997).

Ethical theories of virtue often refer to Aristotle, who described in *Nicomachean Ethics* the human pursuit of happiness through moral excellence. As the name implies, virtue ethics considers character to be important, but virtue ethics also stresses the need for a community that cultivates the virtues. In virtue ethics, moral judgment is seen as something that goes beyond the following of rules. Instead of rules, ethical role models play an important part in developing ethical judgment (Dobson 1997).

An example of such a role model is Warren Buffett, who was viewed by many as the embodiment of integrity when, after the U.S. Treasury auction scandal at Salomon Brothers, he took the helm of the firm in 1991. Buffett immediately stressed the importance of setting an example from the top, and he clarified that he would not tolerate activities "that fall just within the rules" (Hylton 1991).

Thus, in virtue theories, the question, what should I do? is embedded in the question, what sort of person should I be? (Maclagan 1998).

Until recently, virtue ethics was not considered very important in academic efforts to understand ethics in professional business settings because of the tension between its focus on the person and the predominantly problem-oriented thinking of managers. Going beyond specific ethical decisions has gained in importance, however, as skepticism about many management techniques and theories has grown (Maclagan 1998).

3. Psychological and Descriptive Understanding of Ethical Decision Making

The normative approaches to ethical decision making address ideals of how people *should* behave to act ethically. But how many investment professionals truly understand the concept of ethics and are able to knowingly translate it into their actions on a typical workday?

Imagine a recently hired trainee (or even an experienced professional) in an investment firm. A neophyte in the field of ethics but full of good intentions, he wants to stay politically correct in his career and watch his back. He ventures to do some research on the subject. One of the places he hopes to find a concise presentation of how he should behave is in the *Encyclopedia Britannica*. Delighted, he finds an article entitled simply "Ethics." Then, he realizes that the article runs to more than 74 pages and covers an ample mixture of the history of philosophy and world religions. After reading pages on ethical systems from universal prescriptivism to Kant's categorical imperative, the trainee feels more lost than ever.

He soon realizes that encyclopedia articles are long, abstract, and not really practical for his purposes. True enlightenment, he decides, can be found at an ethics seminar. After attending the first class, he is again disappointed. The direction the assigned textbook and the class take is the traditional philosophical one, with the main part dedicated to reviewing the classical normative theories. Although the instructor has adopted some case studies from businesses, theory dominates. But the trainee wants help in dealing with day-to-day practical problems (Hoaglund 1984).

Like this trainee, finance and investment professionals have come to realize that they need more than classical normative theories of ethics to help them in their daily work inside and outside the markets. Fortunately, scholars and researchers have also realized that traditional approaches to ethics have some shortcomings for applying ethics.

The main reason that the normative approaches have limited relevance for the actual world in which investment professionals live is that these theories regard ethical behavior as a detached result of decisions reached by calculating elusive outcomes, applying certain universal principles, or embodying highly abstract virtues. In these approaches, being ethical translates into targeting the ideals prescribed by the classical theories. These ideals are viewed as independent, however, from the psychological processes within the decision maker and from real-life situations and organizational factors that the professionals face.

To be relevant for professionals in the finance and investment industry and to support these professionals in dealing with the complex issues, knowledge from the field of ethics needs to be *practical*. To achieve and to implement this understanding of ethics requires insights from the social sciences, especially from psychology (Brady and Logsdon 1988).

This chapter provides a psychological underpinning for the (un)ethical decisions and behaviors of investment professionals. The sections explain the psychological process of ethical decision making and the psychological stages underlying ethical behavior, describe how investment professionals' perceptions of situations and issues affect their ethics, and explain various psychological influences on the ethics of practitioners' decisions.

The Psychological Process of Ethical Decision Making

A true understanding of people's actual ethical decision making goes beyond the ideals on which normative approaches rest. Thus, many of today's attempts to understand real-life ethics discriminate between *stages* in the ethical decision-making process. These approaches stress that to act ethically, investment professionals have to proceed through a series of steps (Jones 1991; Rest 1986): identify an ethical dilemma, judge what is ethical (a normative dimension), intend to act ethically, and act ethically (Jones, Massey, and Thorne 2003).

1. *Identify an ethical dilemma.* To act ethically, people need to first recognize that there is a moral (i.e., ethical) dimension in a situation. In this phase, they usually first become aware that the situation has an effect on the interests of others. For example, a manager of an investment firm realizes that, although the new incentive system for salespersons may boost the amount of contracts sold by the company, it may eventually harm the interest of customers and jeopardize their trust in the firm. When Sears Roebuck and Co. moved from hourly wages to a compensation system based on the amount of repairs approved by customers, workers at Sears Auto Centers started to tell customers that their cars needed unnecessary repair work. In one investigation, undercover investigators took cars with worn-out brakes but in otherwise perfect condition to the repair shops. Thirty-four of thirty-eight cars were diagnosed by the workers as needing additional repairs (Jennings 2006a). This example shows that being sensitive to the ethical aspects of a situation is especially important when clear, external guidelines, such as professional and organizational rules of conduct, are missing (Jones et al. 2003; Ponemon 1993).

Implicit and unspoken rules of an organization may even actively discourage professionals from recognizing moral issues. In the beginning of the new millennium, 10 leading investment banks were accused of systematically deceiving investors, and they ultimately settled these charges for the sum of US$1.4 billion. During the scandal, a telling statement from a technology research analyst surfaced:

> I have "learned" to adapt to a set of rules that have been imposed by Tech Group banking so as to keep our corporate clients appeased. I believe that these unwritten rules have clearly hindered my ability to be an effective analyst in my various coverage sectors. (Donaldson 2003)

However, although the existence of clear rules and guidelines in the environment can be helpful, finance and investment professionals also differ in their individual capacity to recognize that a situation involves ethical issues. People who are more ethically mature—that is, people at higher stages of individual cognitive moral development—identify ethical issues more easily than people at lower stages do (Sweeney and Roberts 1997).[11] Thus, it may well have been her ethical maturity that allowed Enron Corporation's Sherron Watkins to readily recognize that an ethical issue was involved in some of the company's transactions whereas other employees simply thought that accounting rules made these transactions acceptable.[12]

2. *Judge what is ethical.* After investment professionals recognize that a situation involves an ethical issue, they make a moral judgment about the issue. In other words, they assess the *outcomes* that could result in this particular situation. They decide what *should* be done to resolve the dilemma they face in an ethical way (Jones et al. 2003). For example, the sell-side analyst in a large security firm judges that recommending to downgrade a company would be correct from an ethical viewpoint (Newsome 2005).

3. *Intend to act ethically.* Once investment professionals have made a judgment about what should be done, they then have to establish moral intent. In other words, they have to place their moral concerns ahead of other concerns and interests they may have (such as getting the most money out of a client or getting a quick agreement on a contract), and they have to decide to act on that moral judgment. The analyst who judged that downgrading the company would be the correct thing to do now decides that he will actually downgrade the company, despite his investment banking colleagues' interest in a good recom-

---

[11] *Cognitive moral development* is most closely associated with Lawrence Kohlberg, a moral philosopher and student of child development. Kohlberg observed that growing children advance through definite stages of moral development in a manner similar to their progression through Piaget's well-known stages of cognitive development. This model is discussed further in Chapter 4.
[12] For her testimony, see " 'Lone Voice' " (2002).

mendation and despite the anticipation that he may have to justify himself in uncomfortable confrontations. He may even have to decide to put concerns about potential financial consequences for his personal bonus aside. At this stage, the analyst decides that making an impartial statement and maintaining his professional integrity is more important to him than doing what may lead to less conflict and more financial reward.

4. *Act ethically.* At this stage, people engage in moral behavior according to their intentions. In the case of the financial analyst, the analyst actually submits a recommendation to downgrade the company.

As the example of the financial analyst shows, (un)ethical behavior among professionals in finance and investment is only the visible outcome of a preceding series of psychological steps. Less-than-ethical behavior may be based on a deficit in any of these steps. Differentiating between various stages of ethical decision making helps explain some behavior: Investment professionals do not always recognize that a decision they are about to make has a moral component, their knowing what is morally right does not automatically mean that they intend to do what is morally right, and their intention to do what is morally right is not the same as their acting on that intention (Crane and Matten 2004).

For the analyst in the example, recognizing that his recommendation about the company on which he does research involves aspects of moral right or wrong is only the first step in making an ethical decision. His knowing that it would be right to downgrade the company is different from his intending to personally recommend the downgrade, and although he may intend to downgrade the company, he may still end up not downgrading it.

Perception of Ethical Issues

An important aspect of a psychological understanding of how (un)ethical decisions are made is the individual's perception of the ethical issue itself (Jones 1991). The psychological result of this ethics-focused perception of the issue itself is called "moral intensity," and it has been shown to be a significant influence in ethical decision making.[13] Moral intensity describes the extent to which an issue is perceived as morally important by the decision maker. Moral intensity is high when the importance of the ethical dimension of a situation is crystal clear to the decision maker and when ethical considerations weigh heavily in the mind of the person facing an issue. It is low when the decision maker is hardly aware that the decision has an ethical aspect and when the decision maker proceeds to take action unconstrained by ethical deliberations.

---

[13] Frey (2000); Leitsch (2004); Morris and McDonald (1995); Paolillo and Vitell (2002).

To practitioners in the finance and investment industry, the situations and issues encountered in their professional lives vary widely in terms of their moral intensity. Different factors will determine whether an issue is considered to have a high or low moral intensity. Moral intensity is determined by (implicit) judgments of six aspects of a situation (Jones 1991): magnitude of consequences, social consensus, probability of effect, temporal immediacy, proximity, and concentration of effect.

1. *Magnitude of consequences.* Magnitude addresses the overall harm and benefit that may result from a decision. For example, a fraud scheme that causes thousands of investors to suffer financial losses will be perceived to be of greater magnitude than an act that causes only 10 investors to suffer losses.

2. *Social consensus.* Consensus expresses the degree to which social agreement exists regarding whether a certain act is morally right or wrong. For example, at the time this monograph was being written, a higher degree of social consensus existed in London than in Moscow that kickbacks to secure business with customers are unethical.

3. *Probability of effect.* The likelihood that certain behavior will lead to harm is the "probability of effect." The potentially deceiving "soft language" that is used in securities research can serve as an example. As Newsome (2005) explained, "Securities never fall in price; instead they come 'under pressure.' Financial results are never bad; instead they are 'disappointing.' Or 'less favorable than expected' " (p. 464). When a financial analyst cloaks a negative outlook on a company's stock performance in soft language, the probability of effect of her unethical action depends on how likely it is that investors will be misled by her euphemistic labels.

4. *Temporal immediacy.* How much time lies between the unethical behavior and its harmful consequences? When consequences are in the distant future, people perceive less ethical urgency in the decision they are presently making. For example, for a financial analyst, plagiarizing from a competitor's research report involves less temporal immediacy when the analyst's report is to appear next month than when it will appear tomorrow.

5. *Proximity.* Proximity refers to how psychologically close the decision maker feels to the people who will experience the disadvantage or harm from an unethical decision. For example, front running will involve more proximity for traders when the client to be disadvantaged is somebody seen frequently at social dinners than when the client is anonymous and far away.

6. *Concentration of effect.* Concentration addresses whether the harm will be spread thinly over many people or whether it will affect only a few persons. The effect of cheating only one of a bank's customers out of a given amount of money is more concentrated than if cheating to gain the same amount of money affects

all the bank's customers. For example, a fraudulent transaction from the account of one individual client has a greater concentration of effect than a fraud scheme that is based on incorrectly rounding fractional amounts in all client accounts, even if the resulting overall damage is equal.

Empirical studies indicate that of all the aspects of moral intensity, the first two (magnitude of consequences and social consensus) have the biggest impact on ethical decision making.[14]

When investment professionals make decisions, they determine the moral intensity of a situation or behavior by implicitly evaluating these aspects. The question is, At what point of the decision-making process will their perception of the ethical issue influence them? The moral intensity involved in the perception of ethical issues influences all four stages of moral decision making and behavior (Jones 1991). For example, if an issue has high moral intensity, decision makers will already be more prone to realize that the issue is a moral one than if an issue has low moral intensity. Moreover, issues of high moral intensity elicit more complex moral reasoning and better ethical judgment than do issues of low moral intensity. Finally, an intention to behave ethically will be established more frequently for issues of high moral intensity, as has been shown when professional auditors faced pressure from their clients to misstate information regarding their income (Shafer, Morris, and Ketchand 2001).

In addition to moral intensity, moral *framing* has been identified as an important factor that influences ethical decision making. Moral framing determines the way a situation involving ethical aspects is presented or perceived (Trevino and Nelson 2007). Framing can be likened to looking at the same landscape from various viewpoints: Just as a scene seems different to a spectator who is on a hill and then in a valley, the ethical meaning of a situation and of alternative actions changes according to how the problem and the alternatives are perceived (Slovic 1990).

Consequently, the same ethical problem (in terms of its contents and the objective facts) may lead to radically different behaviors depending merely on the way the problem is described. For example, a financial analyst describing how he "cut and pasted some research parts from elsewhere" provides an innocent frame to his behavior that might also be expressed as, "I stole my colleague's analysis and pretended it was mine in public." Of course, the second way of framing his behavior has a much stronger ethical impact and leads to a different conclusion about its ethical acceptability (Crane and Matten 2004).

Moral framing can be used by financial decision makers to diminish the ethical dimension involved and to justify unethical courses of action. It can also be used by others (for example, superiors) to influence the ethics of others' actions and to downplay the moral implications of their own actions (Trevino and Nelson 2007).

---

[14]Frey (2000); O'Fallon and Butterfield (2005); Reynolds (2006).

Individual, Social, and Organizational/Cultural Factors

Do "bad apples" or "bad barrels" lead to unethical and illegal behavior (Trevino and Youngblood 1990)? To explain ethical misconduct from the bad-apples perspective means taking a *dispositional* approach (i.e., blaming unethical conduct on individuals who are predisposed to behave unethically). From this point of view, what matters are characteristics of the individual and the psychological processes within that individual, such as certain personality traits or the degree of the individual's moral imagination (discussed in Chapter 5 and 6).

Often, however, ethical misconduct can equally well be explained by a bad-barrels perspective, which links unethical behavior to specific ethically disabling situations and organizations to which individuals, regardless of their integrity, succumb (Ashkanasy, Windsor, and Trevino 2006). In such situations, a variety of social factors emerge that affect behavior. Among these factors are conformity (in groups and work teams), obedience, and social influence of interactions between employees and their superiors. Ethically disabling situations may also include a wider organizational context in which decisions are made, such as the culture of the firm and its reward systems. All of these aspects are discussed in Chapters 7–11.

In short, the factors influencing ethical and unethical behavior by finance and investment professionals exist at the individual level, the social context level, and the organizational/cultural level (Frey 2000). Thus, our attention next turns to the impact of psychological mechanisms on these three levels. Traditionally, explanations of ethical decision making have focused either on characteristics of the individual or on the nature of the social and organizational environment. Today, psychology allows examination of these factors not only independently but also in tandem with other factors (Ashkanasy et al. 2006). Although the next chapters present the influences on the ethics of investment professionals separately for the three different levels, all of these factors interact (Trevino 1986) and the distinction between the levels in reality is often blurred. Indeed, exploring the psychology of ethics addresses the interplay of characteristics and behavior at the individual, organizational, and even market level (Dienhart et al. 2001).

4. Individual Ethical Development

This chapter summarizes some of the main psychological insights into how ethics develops in the individual and explains why taking a developmental psychological view is important in understanding ethical attitudes and behavior among investment professionals. The chapter also compares the characteristics of ethically immature and ethically mature persons.

Developmental Psychological View of Ethics

Significant insights into how ethics develops in individuals during their lives are based on the work of psychologist Lawrence Kohlberg. His stage model of ethics sheds light on how people develop and change their ethical convictions and belief systems as they mature psychologically. A predetermined sequence of various stages of moral reasoning determines how people think about ethical issues and how they resolve moral dilemmas. At any given point of their personal development, people are at one ethical stage. As people mature and move up from one stage to the next, their ethical reasoning becomes more thoughtful and simultaneously more complex.

Accordingly, in looking at finance professionals' ethical maturity from the viewpoint of cognitive moral development, the focus is on the reasons these professionals give for what they say is right, not on the actions themselves. In other words, in moral reasoning, it is not the content of the decision that counts but how people arrive at the decision and the reasons they give for making the decision in a certain way (Mudrack 2003).

The moral or ethical reasoning at a trader's or an investment adviser's level of cognitive moral development is by no means a purely academic and abstract affair. Indeed, it may be the most important factor determining practitioners' implicit understanding of what in everyday decisions means "good" and what means "bad" ethically. Also, the level of cognitive moral development has very real consequences for the values that practitioners pursue through their decisions and for the actions they take.

The model of cognitive moral development divides how people reason ethically into three main levels: preconventional, conventional, and principled. Each level consists of two stages.[15]

---

[15]See Colby and Kohlberg (1987); Colby, Lawrence, Gibbs, and Lieberman (1994); Gaudine and Thorne (2001); Kohlberg and Hersh (1977); Kohlberg, Levine, and Hewer (1983); Rest, Turiel, and Kohlberg (1994).

- On the *preconventional* level, individuals think about ethical questions in terms of their own welfare; ethics is based on self-interest. Early on at this level of moral reasoning, individuals define right and wrong simply in relation to external punishments (Stage 1), and later at this level, they define right and wrong on the basis of rewards (Stage 2). In other words, what individuals consider ethically acceptable at this stage is determined by the punishments and rewards attached to possible behavior. In this egoistic "ethics of convenience," individuals behave so as to simply avoid punishment, and in their search for rewards, they may manipulate others (Abdolmohammadi and Sultan 2002). To determine their actions, finance and investment professionals at this level of ethical reasoning implicitly ask, "How can I avoid punishment and not get caught?" or "What rewards can I get out of this?" (Elm and Nichols 1993). Obeying authorities to avoid punishments and being nice to others so they will be nice in return are the guiding reasons at this level for being ethical (Berger and Thompson 1995).

- On the *conventional* level, the expectations of others primarily determine what is considered to be right. Behavior that is consistent with the expectations of others whom the individual deems important is considered to be ethical. In this "ethics of conformity," acceptance and approval by others and loyalty to the social environment are essential (Abdolmohammadi and Sultan 2002). In the early stage of this level (Stage 3), people strive to be good in the sense of being a "good boy" or a "nice girl"; the aim is to please others and win their approval. What is considered ethical behavior in Stage 3 depends on what others praise. Examples of this stage of ethical reasoning are the schoolchild demonstrating against crime to please his teachers or to be praised by his parents and the investment analyst diligently checking his reports to be thought well of by his supervisors. In the later stage of this level of moral reasoning (Stage 4), people determine good and bad in terms of law and order. To be ethical in this stage means to be dutiful and obey society's laws (Berger and Thompson 1995; Elm and Nichols 1993).

- The third level of moral reasoning according to Kohlberg's model is the *principled* or *postconventional* level. Only at this level of individual development do people reach full ethical maturity. In the early stage of this level of moral reasoning (Stage 5), people reason that laws and rules should be followed because they promote the welfare of society. Unlike the straightforward law-and-order orientation of Stage 4, the basic ethical orientation in Stage 5 is based on the notion of a social contract.[16] At this stage, people argue that laws should

---

[16] The term "social contract" originally applied to philosophical theories whose subject is the implied agreements by which people form nations and maintain social order. Prominent advocates of social contract theories were Thomas Hobbes, John Locke, and Jean-Jacques Rousseau.

be followed not simply because they are the law but because these laws are established by mutual agreement and serve the benefit of all in the society. Finally, in Stage 6 of moral reasoning, people develop the capacity to think about ethics independently. They look beyond the social contract; they autonomously develop complex notions of fairness, justice, compassion, equality, and ethical principles (Jolley and Mitchell 1996). The principles address both general justice and individual rights. Stage 6 may be more a theoretical conception than an empirical stage at which people consistently reason morally. In practice, Stage 6 development may manifest itself in an ethical commitment to civil disobedience. Martin Luther King, Jr., arguing that only just laws are valid, disobeyed laws of segregation because he viewed them as unjust (Crain 1985).

To summarize, on the first level of cognitive moral development, decisions are based on pure self-interest. On the second level, people base their decisions on a desire for approval and on a wish to avoid disapproval. On the third level, people view ethical decisions in terms of society's welfare. These levels of cognitive moral development reflect progress from childhood to adulthood. Moreover, they define important differences between ethically immature and ethically mature adults and professionals (Kegan 1982).

Kohlberg claimed that moral development occurs as people actively and mindfully encounter ethical challenges. Development is supported through dialogue and common reflection with others on situations and issues involving ethical questions and through confrontations with different points of view. Thus, the theory of cognitive moral development has important implications for efforts to educate and train investment professionals in ethics. A typical issue would be, Is it ethically legitimate to accept gifts from customers? What kinds of gifts? In what role? Under which circumstances? For practitioners to understand the ethical issues involved and correctly navigate such critical questions, practitioners' ethical reasoning process needs to be developed. Although learning the "correct" response by heart may help finance professionals mindlessly do the right thing in a particular situation, such learning leads to little personal progress or genuine ethical maturity. For this reason, identifying a practitioner's ethical maturity simply on the basis of the person "knowing the right solution" can be misleading; people can arrive at identical conclusions about what should be done by using different moral reasoning processes. Moreover, a person may be unable to even understand another approach to resolving an ethical issue because the person's low level of moral reasoning does not allow them to comprehend the values and reasoning involved in a higher-level solution (Jolley and Mitchell 1996). In short, individual moral development does not result from telling people what to think in terms of content or how to "correctly" resolve a moral issue but from teaching them how to reason ethically.

Assessment of Moral Reasoning

To determine a person's level of ethical maturity, psychologists use moral dilemmas that pit the person's values against each other. In one famous example of such a dilemma, people are told about Heinz, whose wife is seriously ill with cancer and close to death. A pharmacist has invented a cure for the disease but charges twice the amount Heinz can borrow from others. The pharmacist will not sell the drug more cheaply. Getting desperate, Heinz breaks in to the pharmacist's store and steals the drug.

When people think about and discuss whether the husband should have stolen the drug, they use moral reasoning, which allows psychologists to identify the levels of ethical maturity of the people. The nature of their moral reasoning is shown not as much in their actual conclusions regarding the rightness of Heinz's actions as it is in the reasons and explanations that they give for why Heinz should act in a certain way.

Why are reasons and explanations so important? They are important because people at different levels of moral reasoning may reach the same conclusion. Moreover, the same level of moral reasoning may lead individuals to *different* conclusions. For example, a person in Stage 2 of the preconventional level, where ethical reasoning is guided by possible rewards for good behavior, may support the stealing of the drug by saying that if Heinz happens to be caught, he can return the drug and probably will receive a lenient sentence. Another person on exactly the same level of moral reasoning may reject the theft by reasoning that, although the expected sentence may be short, Heinz's wife will have died before he gets out of prison (Jolley and Mitchell 1996; Selman 1976).

Suppose Heinz is an investment professional who is considering taking money from a company account to pay for his brother's kidney operation. Or suppose Heinz is a financial officer who finds himself caught in the quandary of whether to report a misdeed of his supervisor, the chief financial officer of the company and the loving father of four small children, whom he has always perceived to be a dutiful and supportive company man and a real asset to the company?

Suppose this financial officer, named Debra, chooses to follow the company's rule for handling this misconduct: She reports her supervisor to the authorities. Does her decision reveal whether she is ethically mature in a psychological sense and at which level of moral development she is? No, it does not. To answer those questions, we need to know more about Debra's reasons for choosing to obey the rule. Depending on her ethical maturity, Debra might base her behavior on vastly different ethical reasoning, as shown in **Exhibit 1** (see Jolley and Mitchell 1996).

Assessing the moral reasoning of finance and investment professionals and understanding their professional ethics from this developmental psychological perspective provide an important perspective on (un)ethical conduct and decisions. A large number of research studies has shown that cognitive moral development is positively correlated with ethical decision making (e.g., O'Fallon and Butterfield 2005). Finance professionals who engage in unethical behavior may do so not because their behavior expresses stable personality characteristics that are part of their unchangeable nature; their behavior may be based on convictions about what the situations call for and what being ethical means. Their reasoning when they communicate their convictions about ethical issues reveals their current stance in a process of psychological development and maturation.

How ethics develops over the life of an individual can be compared with how systems of justice and fairness have developed in the history of mankind. For example, the Old Testament's retribution law "an eye for an eye" seems inhumane and cruel in Western cultures today. From a historical viewpoint, however, this law can be understood as an early stage in the development of Western legal systems over the centuries. Similarly, unethical actions by investment professionals may reflect an immature stage in the individual's cognitive moral development.

Exhibit 1. Debra's Possible Reasons

Level of Cognitive Moral Development	Possible Underlying Reasoning
Preconventional	
Stage 1	I follow the company rule so I will not get punished.
Stage 2	If I report him, doing so will pay off some later day.
Conventional	
Stage 3	If I report him, my colleagues will approve of me because I acted professionally.
Stage 4	I have to report him because it is the law.
Postconventional	
Stage 5	I follow the rule because the rule was established in the interest of all company members and because following the rule is the right thing to do for society at large.
Stage 6	I follow the rule because the rule is based on universal principles with which I agree. I would not follow the rule if I did not agree with it.

5. Ethics-Related Individual Characteristics

"We are the good guys. We are on the side of angels," Jeffrey Skilling once remarked (quoted in Jennings 2005, p. 51). In stark contrast to the idea expressed in this quotation about financial professionals, personalities in the investment industry have not always been portrayed in a flattering light in Hollywood productions—think of Gordon Gekko (played by actor Michael Douglas in the 1987 film *Wall Street*) or Patrick Bateman (portrayed by actor Christian Bale in the 2000 movie *American Psycho*). And although these fictional characters often seem exaggerated, the imagination of movie producers has apparently been stimulated by real-life events and personalities (Hartikainen and Torstila 2004).

For example, take Skilling himself, once chief executive officer of Enron Corporation. He was found guilty of securities fraud and sentenced to more than 20 years in prison. Another striking example is Michael Smirlock, a highly talented holder of a PhD in finance, who at a young age was already a professor at the Wharton School of the University of Pennsylvania and a partner at Goldman Sachs. During the ascent of what seemed to be a brilliant and extraordinarily successful professional career, he was fined by the U.S. Securities and Exchange Commission and forced to resign for dubious late-trade allocations. With a highly publicized scandal already on his track record, he established various hedge funds and was caught again. He received a four-year prison sentence and was fined more than US$10 million for committing fraud by concealing losses from his investors (Bernstein 2006; Lux 1998).

In addition to cognitive moral development, the crucial importance of which was discussed in the previous chapter, a large number of other individual psychological factors help explain unethical and ethical behavior in the world of finance and investment. This chapter discusses some of the most important ethics-related characteristics of the individual.[17] In scope, it ranges from personality traits to differences in individuals' capacity for moral imagination.

---

[17] In addition to the psychological and personality-related individual factors discussed in this chapter, a number of other individual variables have been empirically studied for their possible effects on ethical behavior. These variables include gender, age, religion, education, and employment status (Ford and Richardson 1994; Loe, Ferrell, and Mansfield 2000; O'Fallon and Butterfield 2005).

Machiavellianism and Integrity

"Greed . . . is good. Greed is right. Greed works. Greed clarifies, cuts through, and captures the essence of the evolutionary spirit." So declares character Gordon Gekko in the movie *Wall Street*. Almost the same words were uttered, in precisely the same spirit, by trader Ivan Boesky, who played a leading role in the Wall Street insider-trading scandal of the mid-1980s. He declared in a speech to graduates of the University of California at Berkeley, "Greed is healthy. You can be greedy and still feel good about yourself."[18] Not long afterward, he was jailed and received a fine of US$100 million for the trading violations.

Some observers have explained Boesky's and others' high esteem for greed, their unethical behavior, and the shrewd tactics they used to make money by referring to their personalities. Two personality traits are particularly relevant to the ethics of the decisions people make and to the behaviors they engage in: Machiavellianism and integrity.

Machiavellianism is a term for the tendency to deceive and manipulate others for personal gain.[19] Machiavellian personalities are highly manipulative, pragmatic, and persuasive; they believe that whatever means are needed to achieve a desired end are justified (Christie and Geis 1970). Empirical studies have consistently shown that a high degree of Machiavellianism leads to less-than-ethical decisions (O'Fallon and Butterfield 2005). The MACH-IV, a widely available personality test to assess Machiavellianism, indicates that people who score high in Machiavellianism are power oriented and calculating with others. They do not shy away from manipulating others to pursue their goals by using deceptive tactics or insincere promises. People who score low in Machiavellianism are more open in their interactions with others and more trusting in the good intentions of others.

Also, *integrity* has been found to be a central personality aspect of participants in financial markets (Oberlechner 2004a). Integrity can be defined as "adherence to moral principles or values" (Crane and Matten 2004, p. 123). It is a combination of personal virtues that are meaningfully embedded in something that goes beyond the individual person (i.e., in society and the human community). This description may sound rather esoteric and philosophical, but integrity is a deeply practical basis for a life lived decently (Solomon 1999), and the prominent role of integrity has become visible especially in times of ethical crises. For example, under the leadership of Warren Buffett, personal integrity became the key for restructuring Salomon Brothers. Buffett, declaring that he would "fire anyone flirting with impropriety"

---

[18] The story of Boesky and other real-life traders involved in the scandal, such as Michael Milken, Martin Siegel, and Dennis Levine, is recounted in *Den of Thieves* by Pulitzer Prize winning author James B. Stewart (1991).

[19] Niccolò Machiavelli, a 15th century Italian politician and statesman, is best known (perhaps unfairly) for a pamphlet he wrote, *The Prince*, to gain acceptance by the Medici family of Florence. The pamphlet lays out how a strong (ruthless, deceptive, and cruel) individual leader should behave.

("Cleaning Up Salomon's Mess" 1991), happily announced that he would let employees go who were dissatisfied with the new focus on integrity and promised added opportunities to those employees who shared his values (see also Eichenwald 1991). Regarding the importance of integrity, Buffett remarked, "In evaluating people, you look for three qualities: integrity, intelligence and energy. If you don't have the first, the other two will kill you" (Hagstrom 2005, p. 102).

Psychological Attributions and Locus of Control

The ethics of individuals is affected by the causes they perceive for their own and for others' behavior and by the extent to which they consider themselves in control of their own actions.

Attribution. *Attributions* are the judgments people make about the causes of behavior and events. People form attributions all the time in order to understand their experience and to find causal explanations of what happens in their environment.

Attributions are important psychological processes in the ethics of individuals. They can be illustrated by an example from the collapse of Barings Bank in 1995. At that time, the British bank had successfully operated for more than a century and was considered one of the most prestigious financial institutions in the world. Then, by trying to extricate himself from previous losses through increasingly frenetic deals, a single trader in Singapore accumulated more than £800 million of trading losses. Nick Leeson, the trader behind the losses, was jailed and later recounted his story in a tell-all book entitled *Rogue Trader: How I Brought Down Barings Bank and Shook the Financial World* (Leeson 1996).

But what *really* was responsible for the fall of Barings Bank? An attempt to answer this question leads right into the psychology of attribution. This topic is at the heart of how ethical individuals perceive themselves to be and how ethical others perceive them to be. When people form an *internal* attribution, their psychological perception of a situation holds the actor responsible for certain behavior or a certain event. When they form an *external* attribution, they hold situational causes responsible. Seeing Leeson (i.e., his personality and his reckless risk taking) as responsible for the Barings Bank disaster is an example of an internal attribution. In contrast, holding missing bank regulations and supervisory failure responsible exemplifies an external attribution.

Attributions play a particularly important role in the assignment of responsibility for ethical and unethical behavior. For example, a moral reproach requires that we see somebody's freely performed actions as harmful to others (Velasquez and Rostankowski 1985). Considering an action (our own behavior or somebody else's behavior) unethical presupposes that we see the actor as being responsible for the action (an internal attribution). When external factors determine an unethical action, we do not see the person as unethical.

The way people form attributions is biased; it does not necessarily correspond to objective reality or to actual reasons for behavior and events. Systematic and predictable psychological biases regularly distort to which factors we attribute our own and others' unethical behavior. For example, when people make judgments about the causes of behavior, they generally underestimate situational factors and overestimate individual factors (Ross and Anderson 1982). In other words, people usually hold persons, not situations, responsible. Psychologists call this phenomenon the "fundamental attribution error."

Moreover, unethical behavior may be perceived very differently by the actors themselves than by outside observers (Payne and Giacalone 1990; Ross and DiTecco 1975). Individuals, including professionals in finance and investment, have a tendency to credit themselves for their ethical decisions but to blame situational forces imposed by the environment for their unethical decisions (Payne and Giacalone). This bias is called the "self-serving attribution bias."

The fundamental attribution error and the self-serving attribution bias may have crucial effects on ethics-related decisions. These psychological processes may lead us to draw the wrong conclusions about the causes of unethical behavior or find "solutions" to ethical difficulties that do not reach the true, underlying problem. For example, the vice president of product sales at an investment firm realizes that some members of the sales force for a particular new financial product have engaged in grossly unethical sales tactics. To reach their sales quotas, some of the salespeople have not fully informed customers about the risks of the product and have deliberately withheld information about alternative, less risky products. The vice president of product sales, succumbing to the fundamental attribution error, holds the overly ambitious and overly aggressive personality of the head of sales responsible for this unethical behavior. He decides to demote the head of sales and put a new person in this position. A year later, he realizes that the unethical sales practices are in full bloom again. He had not thought about the possibility that the nature of the organizational bonus system might lead anybody in the position of head of sales to develop overly aggressive and unethical sales practices for a new product.

The Psychological Locus of Control. In addition to these universal attribution biases in how professionals view the behavior of others, their attributions about their *own* actions may be biased by their personal attribution styles. Does a person believe she is in control of her destiny or that an external force (e.g., some other powerful person) is in control? Whether a person tends to attribute causes of events to external forces or to internal sources defines the *psychological locus of control* (Rotter 1966). Individuals with an internal locus of control accept responsibility for a high degree of personal control over their lives and over the outcomes of their actions, whereas individuals with an external locus of control attribute the events in their lives to luck or other people.

The locus of control plays an important role in whether and how investment professionals are willing to engage in ethical behavior (Trevino and Nelson 2007; Trevino and Youngblood 1990). People with an internal locus of control tend to accept more ethical responsibility; they are morally more mature, they behave more ethically, and they resist social pressures that contradict their own ethical standards.[20] People with an external locus of control will tend to depend on others to decide which behavior is acceptable and tend to view factors that are beyond their control as being responsible for their actions (Forte 2005; Trevino 1986).

Examples of an external locus of control may be found among some of the financial analysts who recommended buying Enron's stock even as the company's fortunes turned sour. In the aftermath of the company's collapse, these analysts denied any personal accountability for their costly advice, maintaining that they had been unaware because they had no choice but to rely on Enron's bookkeeping without questioning anything. Others ask, "Why didn't these analysts press for answers or see the lack of information as a warning sign?" (Oppel 2002).

Moral Imagination

In addition to Machiavellianism versus integrity and how one makes attributions and assigns blame, another important individual characteristic linked to ethical decisions and behavior is *moral imagination*—the ability to perceive a variety of options for behavior in a situation and to imagine the positive or negative consequences of those options (Johnson 1993). In short, moral imagination is a person's imaginative awareness of a wide range of decision possibilities together with their respective moral consequences.[21]

People with a high degree of moral imagination can reflect on decisions with moral implications in more than one fixed way; they can think of these decisions flexibly in various ways. For instance, Joseph Jett was a 36-year-old trader in charge of government bonds at the securities firm Kidder, Peabody, & Co. In 1993, Jett earned a bonus of more than US$9 million. One year later, he was dismissed for the fraudulent trading activities he had engaged in to artificially boost his firm's trading profits and, consequently, his own bonus (Hansell 1994). What allowed him to act this way?

Some people attributed his wrongdoing simply to greed, but this answer falls short of a full explanation of Jett's unethical actions.[22] Instead of greed, Jett may have had a low degree of moral imagination. A lack of moral imagination may have

---

[20]Johnson, Ackerman, and Frank (1968); Lefcourt (1976); Murk and Addleman (1992); O'Fallon and Butterfield (2005); Trevino and Youngblood (1990).
[21]Pardales (2002); Vidaver-Cohen (1998); Werhane (1998); Williams (1998).
[22]This attribution was made by Paul Volcker, who was chairman of the U.S. Federal Reserve Board at that time (Bacon and Salwen 1991).

allowed him to understand his professional activities in one fixed way—namely, in terms of making as much money as possible—and to limit his moral deliberations. Jett may have visualized little connection between (1) general moral considerations and the ethical principles he lived by outside his trading profession and (2) what he was doing at his workplace (Werhane 1998).

In short, the concept of moral imagination addresses the flexibility with which finance and investment professionals perceive the so-called unchangeable realities of their work life. Having moral imagination permits them to "see beyond the rules of the game that seem to be operating in the workplace" and to develop a larger picture of the moral issues and of the effects of their professional behavior (Crane and Matten 2004, p. 126).

The capacity for moral imagination has played a role in cinema. In the 1982 science fiction thriller *Blade Runner*, a test is used to determine whether somebody is a "replicant" (i.e., an android) or a human. The test measures such reactions as eye dilation in response to certain scenarios (such as the following) that in true humans evoke feelings and empathy: *"You're in a desert, walking along in the sand, when all of the sudden you look down and you see a tortoise. You reach down; you flip the tortoise over on its back. The tortoise lies on its back, its belly baking in the hot sun, beating its legs, trying to turn itself over, but it can't, not without your help, but you're not helping."*

Leon, one of the replicants in the film, does not pass the test, but people with moral imagination would. Empathy (i.e., the ability to put oneself in other people's shoes and understand what they experience from their point of view) is an important basis of moral imagination. This ability allows us to understand what is good from the perspective of the community and of society, rather than basing what is good purely on egoistic values and interests (Werhane 1998).

6. Implicit Individual Processes

As a follow-up to Chapter 5's discussion of the ethics-related characteristics of the individual, this chapter explains some of the most important psychological *processes* in the individual that influence ethics. These processes include attitudes, decision heuristics, cognitive dissonance reduction, rationalization strategies, moral disengagement, and such affects as shame and guilt. Psychological processes may inspire and support unethical behavior, or they may be a consequence of unethical behavior. Although these processes regularly operate on an implicit and unconscious level (thus influencing decisions and behavior outside a decision maker's awareness), they can also show that no clear demarcation line exists between unconscious and conscious dynamics in individual ethics.

Attitudes

When asked whether they consider themselves ethical in their professional conduct, most investment professionals will reply without hesitation that they do. Indeed, nearly everyone is convinced that he or she is ethical. Implicit and unconscious psychological processes, however, may distort the decisions and the behavior of even the most considerate and conscientious person. So, actual ethical behavior may be in contradiction to espoused values (Argyris, Putnam, and Smith 1985; Diamond and Adams 1999), and one's perception of ethical standards may be different from objective reality (Banaji, Bazerman, and Chugh 2003). In fact, research shows that professionals rate their own ethical behavior better than they rate the behavior of their coworkers (Morgan 1993).

Readers who now think that, although this discrepancy may be true for others, it does not apply to them personally are encouraged to interrupt their reading for a few minutes to take one of various "association tests" made available online by psychologists Brian Nosek, Mahzarin Banaji, and Tony Greenwald (https://implicit.harvard.edu/implicit). These tests reveal implicit biases and stereotypes in attitudes based on the speed of the test takers' associations between positively and negatively charged words and various groups of people. The researchers have found that the biases are not only widespread and stable but they also work independently of good intentions. (Many readers who take the tests will be surprised to find they themselves are biased.) Implicit subjective biases concern not only prejudice regarding gender, race, and religion but also biases that favor any group to which we belong, and they play an important role when conflicts of interest lead us unconsciously to give preference to the people from whom we think we can benefit (Banaji et al. 2003).

Whether investment professionals are aware of it or not, attitudes play a leading role in the ethics of the decisions they make. Psychologists have shown that when people react to situations and events, they first form a spontaneous, overall, affective judgment (is this good or is this bad for me?) before they evaluate the situation in a more comprehensive and thoughtful way (Zajonc 2000; Zajonc and Markus 1982). Conscious and unconscious attitudes have a significant influence on the resulting decisions and behavior because these attitudes influence the perceptions and thoughts involved in the process (Fazio 1986; Fazio and Towles-Schwen 1999).

Examples of how implicit attitudes influence professionals' decisions and lead to unintended unethical behavior include unfair hiring decisions, biased dealings with colleagues within one's own organization, and giving preferential treatment to certain groups of customers while discriminating against others.

Decision Heuristics

Another psychological process that influences the ethical decision making of individuals is the use of *decision heuristics*. Cognitive psychologists have shown that when making decisions, people generally do not process the available information in a comprehensive way. Instead, they use heuristics; that is, they reduce and simplify the existing information by using psychological shortcuts and rules of thumb (Dreman 1995). These heuristics usually work automatically; the decision makers are not usually aware of the heuristics' existence and how the heuristics influence their decisions. Particularly relevant to finance and investment professionals is the fact that heuristics are especially important when decisions are made in complex situations and when they need to be made rapidly. In such cases, heuristics limit the amount of information that needs to be processed and thus the cognitive demands on the professional (Duchon, Ashmos, and Dunegan 1991; Gigerenzer and Todd 1999).

Although decision heuristics often produce high-quality judgments by expediting and simplifying decision making, they may also produce systematic mistakes (Hogarth 1981; Tversky and Kahneman 1974). For example, when finance professionals use the so-called *availability heuristic*, they judge the likelihood of an event (for example, the chances of the Japanese yen going up or the chances of the chief financial officer leaking inside information before a major company acquisition is announced) by the psychological availability of information. Application of the availability heuristic leads them to assign far greater likelihoods to events for which information is psychologically easily accessible (i.e., a similar instance or event is easy to bring to mind) than to events that are harder to imagine. The availability heuristic often leads to accurate judgments but may also be an inadequate way to judge the likelihood of events because the recollection of events is sometimes determined by factors that have little to do with the actual frequency of such events (Tversky and Kahneman 1973). For example, infrequent events, such as a major market crash, may be easily "available" because they are prominently covered in the news, because we perceive them as emotionally relevant, and because they are vivid and sensational (Plous 1993). Nevertheless, in any given period, they are improbable.

As these examples suggest, many of the decision-making heuristics identified by psychologists are at work when people assess probabilities and engage in quasi-mathematical reasoning (Strudler and Warren 2001). Heuristics may influence ethical decisions by the way they "edit" the decision alternatives for someone facing an ethical choice. When heuristics cause us to neglect or underweight information that would have led to an ethical choice, heuristics work against ethical decision making. For example, the availability heuristic may have played an important role in the drug producers' decision to continue to sell DES (diethylstilbestrol, a synthetic estrogen), which was prescribed to pregnant women during the 1950s, 1960s, and early 1970s mainly to prevent miscarriage and which was found to cause serious birth defects. The idea that the drug would not harm the consumers themselves but the children of the consumers may simply not have been a readily "available" idea to the producers (Messick and Bazerman 2001).

Nonstatistical decision heuristics also influence (un)ethical decisions. One example is the *equality heuristic* (see Messick 1993), which is at work when people try to make fair decisions about how to allocate resources and rewards and when people strive for fairness by using a straightforward concept of equality (that is, treating everybody identically). Another example is the *authority heuristic*. When people use this heuristic, they simply rely on the judgment of a perceived authority or defer to the judgment of an expert to save the time and cognitive effort involved in establishing an independent judgment. Using this heuristic is often rational and pragmatic, such as when a patient accepts the dentist's proposal for a root canal (Strudler and Warren 2001) or a junior analyst rewrites his company report according to the suggestions of an experienced supervisor. Relying on this heuristic may also lead to dramatically unethical behavior, however, as will be shown in Chapter 7.

Cognitive Dissonance Reduction

What do people who act unethically do to justify their behavior to themselves and to others? A convincing answer to this question is provided by the concept of *cognitive dissonance reduction* (Festinger 1957). Cognitive dissonance arises when decision makers hold contradictory perceptions of, attitudes toward, or evaluations of something. Most importantly, cognitive dissonance results when people realize they are behaving inconsistently with their evaluation. For example, people who like to smoke cigarettes may also know that smoking causes cancer; they thus experience cognitive dissonance. A positive perception ("smoking tastes good") contradicts a negative evaluation ("smoking is bad for my health").

Because cognitive dissonance creates an uncomfortable psychological tension, people try to reduce it or get rid of it. Smokers, for example, may attempt to change their behavior—either by reducing or quitting smoking. Another strategy to reduce cognitive dissonance is to change a conflicting perception or evaluation. Smokers may convince themselves that smoking may not be dangerous after all. Thus, unpleasant cognitive dissonance can be reduced by a change in behavior or by a change in attitude (Starmer 1993).

Finance and investment professionals will experience cognitive dissonance when they plan to engage in actions they know to be unethical or when they have already done something unethical. In these cases, because the professionals generally think of themselves as ethical and believe that others are less ethical (Tyson 1990), they will experience cognitive dissonance ("I am an ethical person, but I am doing something unethical") and try to reduce the resulting tension. One way to do so is, of course, to not engage in the unethical action or to stop engaging in it and make up for the harm caused to others.

Psychological "tricks" are also available, however, that allow individuals to continue their unethical course of action while reducing cognitive dissonance. One such trick is for the person to form a perception of the situation in which her behavior is no longer at odds with her self-image. For instance, she may come to see her action as no longer actively unethical but as a justified defense, one in which she must engage, or as something that is not unethical after all. For example, a salesperson at an investment company who is using dishonest sales tactics with his customers may remind himself of an instance when he felt tricked by a customer and think, I want to make sure I do not get cheated again. Or he may think of his family and explain his behavior to himself as a sign of a good father who makes sure his children can afford college tuition.

Another way to reduce cognitive dissonance is to change one's self-image from somebody who is innocent and naive to somebody who simply understands how to "play the game" successfully. An example of how cognitive dissonance can change ethical thinking and the self-image of professionals is the following recollection of the thought processes of a novice salesperson: He realizes that he has been tricked into selling unprofitable bonds to his client by a veteran colleague, thus risking the customer's financial well-being and his good relationship with the customer. When selling the bonds, the novice had actually thought he was acting in his customer's interest because he followed the recommendation of a senior and well-informed colleague. Later, he finds out that his colleague, a trader, only wanted to get rid of the bank's own unpromising bonds:

> I had actually thought that the customer was going to make money. . . . How could anyone be so stupid as to trust a trader? The best thing I could do was to pretend to others . . . that I had meant to screw the customer. People would respect that. (Lewis 1989, p. 167)

The cognitive dissonance caused by the tension among (1) his need for recognition, (2) his self-definition of being trustworthy, and (3) his realization of having abused the trust of a customer quickly changed this novice's self-definition to that of a ruthless trader who would cold-bloodedly dump unprofitable bonds on unsuspecting customers (Darley 2001).

A study of unfair competition and personal gains showed that a manager's moral development significantly influences the intensity of cognitive dissonance experienced by a manager (Lii 2001). Thus, strategies for reducing cognitive dissonance after unethical behavior may be especially important for investment professionals in the higher stages of cognitive moral development (see Chapter 3).

Rationalization and Moral Disengagement

Sometimes, professionals with generally high ethical standards of morality engage in highly immoral acts. For others, realizing such aberrations in the behavior of somebody they have known, liked, and trusted can be a shocking experience and is often accompanied by disbelief that it actually could happen. Take, for example, the behavior of Kenneth Lay. As of this writing, his website was still describing him as the loving father of five children, as a dedicated professional who served on the board of dozens of civic and philanthropic associations, as one who received countless awards and honors, and as one who, together with his wife of 23 years, donated money to hundreds of not-for-profit organizations.[23] A former chairman and chief executive officer (CEO) of Enron Corporation, Lay was found guilty on multiple counts of conspiracy, fraud, and false statements in 2006. Lay died of coronary artery disease before being sentenced to what could have been decades in prison (Pasha 2006; Pasha and Seid 2006).

How professionals end up in the midst of an ethical dilemma where they compromise their sense of ethics can be explained by the efforts we make to rationalize our behavior. The language used in these efforts includes such lines of defense as "that's the way they do it here," "that's the way it has always been done," "I was simply following orders" (see Chapter 7), "for all I do around here, I deserve this," "everybody else does it," and "it doesn't really hurt anyone" (Jennings 1998, p. 18ff).

How otherwise highly ethical professionals end up compromising their ethics can be explained in depth by the psychological process by which people morally "disengage" from their behavior.[24] People use four main cognitive strategies to morally disengage from their behavior. The strategies aim to change (1) the person's

---

[23]The website is www.kenlayinfo.com.
[24]Moral disengagement was described by social psychologist Albert Bandura (see Bandura 1988; Bandura, Barbaranelli, Caprara, and Pastorelli 1996; Beu and Buckley 2004; Osofsky, Bandura, and Zimbardo 2005).

perception of the unethical behavior, (2) the person's perception of the damaging consequences, (3) awareness of being responsible, and (4) perspectives on the *victim* (Zimbardo 2004, 2007).

- *Change in perception of the unethical behavior.* This change is achieved by moral justifications for behavior, by putting euphemistic labels on the unethical behavior, or by making soothing comparisons. An example is the inexperienced novice salesman who involuntarily learns to trick small investors into buying unprofitable bonds from his banks' trading books (Lewis 1989). For the deceit, his colleagues use such justifying euphemisms as "jamming" bonds, which suggests alternative interpretations of their unethical strategies by implicitly allowing them to feel like a competitive sports team (Darley 2001).
- *Change in perception of the damaging consequences of the unethical behavior.* This change is achieved by completely closing one's eyes to the consequences, by playing down the consequences, or by distorting the consequences. An example is given in former WorldCom CEO Bernie Ebbers' declaration, "You'll see people who in the early days . . . took their savings and trusted this company with their money. And I have an awesome responsibility to those people to make sure that they're doing right" (Jennings 2005, p. 51). In 2005, Ebbers was convicted of fraud and conspiracy. WorldCom's false financial reporting caused billions of dollars of losses to investors.
- *Change in awareness of being responsible for the connection between the blameworthy behavior and its damaging consequences.* This change is achieved by displacing responsibility onto others or by diffusing responsibility among many. Such diffusion of responsibility may be found, for instance, when highly unethical organizational norms develop. In the case of one investment bank, for example, derivatives traders collectively came to feel that it was fine to "rip the face off" (Partnoy 1997, p. 61) customers by making them buy from the bank's proprietary accounts stocks and bonds that were about to collapse (see also Dunfee 2001).
- *Change in perspective on the victims of the unethical behavior.* This change is achieved by dehumanizing the victim—even putting the blame on the victim. For example, investment professionals at Hampton Porter Investment Bankers lured unsuspecting investors into purchasing certain penny stocks and then sold the firm's own stocks of these companies at the unsuspecting investors' expense (Department of Justice 2003). To justify their illegal deception to themselves, the professionals may well have thought of the investors not in terms of "this person is my customer" but in terms of "this stupid crowd harassing me in my work life deserves to be taught a lesson if it asks for it."

These examples show the wide range of psychological mechanisms that allow investment professionals to diminish the unpleasant feelings of shame and guilt that come along with perceiving oneself as unethical.

Shame and Guilt

Feelings of shame and guilt serve a dual function for ethical behavior: They can inhibit and prevent people from engaging in unethical behavior, and they are common reactions of ethical individuals who engage in unethical behavior. Ever since Sigmund Freud, psychoanalysts have stressed that shame and guilt may be experienced on a conscious level, where the person is aware of experiencing the feelings, and on a unconscious level, outside the person's awareness but nonetheless influencing the person.

Unconscious shame and guilt may lead a person to engage in acts or in continued patterns of behavior without being aware of the actual motives for the behavior. For example, the CEO of an investment company who has abused his company's travel account for a leisure trip with his partner may be surprised to find himself (because of unconscious shame) giving generous gifts to his employees at the end of the year, and he may explain his actions to himself as resulting from his "generosity."

Although shame and guilt are often used interchangeably in everyday conversations, a clear distinction exists between them. Shame is an inhibition of, or reaction to, unacceptable behavior to avoid external punishment. Guilt is an inhibition of, or reaction to, unacceptable behavior that is caused by one's own conscience (i.e., because internal moral standards are violated) (see Corcoran and Rotter 1987). This difference has important implications: Regarding their unethical behavior, people who are motivated primarily by shame, not by guilt, will simply attempt to avoid "getting caught" and will stop the unethical behavior only when they feel at risk of being found out (Corcoran and Rotter).

7. Social Influences on Ethics

When evaluating professional decisions and behavior in the finance and investment industry, high standards of ethics and blatant violations of ethical conventions are difficult to explain solely in terms of individual traits and personality. Situational factors may lead to considerable differences in the ethical standards of behavior of a single individual in different social situations—a fact that has been revealed time and again by media reports. Thus, a true understanding of the psychology of ethics in the world of finance and investment requires awareness of how people interact and influence each other ethically.

This chapter starts by providing psychological insights into the extent to which social influence may affect the ethical behavior of individuals; people can *radically* influence others' ethical decision making. The chapter then discusses how people influence others' ethics in professional relationships. The chapter concludes by discussing the widespread use of "impression management" to control the ethics-related impressions of others.

Toward Evil: Social Psychology of Unethical Behavior

The dramatic extent to which situational factors can influence ethical decision making has been shown by social psychology experiments in which ordinary people administer what they believe to be extremely painful and life-threatening electric shocks to others or in which they quickly take on the role of psychologically cruel and sadistic prison guards.[25] The results of this research demonstrate how powerfully role expectations and the demands of a situation determine the ethical behavior of people. As Brady and Logsdon (1988) discussed, these results are most relevant for finance and investment professionals.

In the first experiment, social psychologist Stanley Milgram examined whether ordinary people could be induced by a perceived authority to commit unethical deeds they would never commit when alone (see Milgram 1963, 1974).[26] In Milgram's experiments, ordinary people who were encountered on the street were invited to participate in a study allegedly about memory and learning. Their task was to administer electric shocks to a "learner" when he made mistakes in remembering

---

[25] See Gibson, Haritos-Fatouros, Milgram, and Bushman (1991); Haney, Banks, and Zimbardo (1973); Milgram (1963, 1964); Zimbardo (1995, 2004, 2007).

[26] His interest in blind obedience to authority was fueled by the 1945–49 Nuremberg trials of Nazi leaders. At the trials, ordinary citizens and loving fathers of families responded to the question of why they had actively participated in the horror of the Holocaust by saying that they were merely following orders (Peterson 2001).

word pairs. This learner was supposedly an older man who mentioned at the beginning of the experiment that he had a heart condition. Hooked up to electric wires, he was seated in a separate room. The participants invited from the street did not know that the role of the learner was being performed by a professional actor and that, in reality, the wires were not connected to any electrical system.

Whenever the learner made a memory mistake, the participants were instructed to administer increasingly intense electric shocks. At 75 volts, the learner started to moan. At 150 volts, the learner demanded to be released from the experiment. At 180 volts, he cried out loudly that he could not bear the pain any more. At 300 volts, while crying out, he called attention to his heart problems and insisted on being released from the experiment immediately. Whenever the participant hesitated to provide further shocks to the learner, the experimenter, an official-looking man in a white laboratory coat, said, "The experiment requires that you continue," or "You have no other choice; you *must* go on."

The results of this experiment are disturbing. The majority of participants fully complied with the instructions of the experimenter and continued to provide shocks up to the maximum voltage of 450 volts. No single participant stopped below 300 volts. Also, although many participants tried to verbally resist the commands of the authority, only a few actually stopped providing electric shocks (Gerrig and Zimbardo 2005).

The content of the task assigned to the participants in this study may seem irrelevant to the activities of investment professionals. The basic situation, however—following a supervisor's instructions that are clearly unethical—is decidedly relevant.

Insights from social psychology research on the power of social roles are equally relevant, as shown in the so-called Stanford Prison Experiment. Social psychologist Philip Zimbardo investigated the powerful influence of situational factors on human behavior by placing ordinary people in a simulated prison in the basement of Stanford University's psychology building (Zimbardo 2007). Based on careful screening, researchers selected the 24 most psychologically stable of 75 male applicants and assigned them randomly either to the role of prisoner or to the role of prison guard. Besides being informed of their roles and receiving uniforms, dark sunglasses, and a general assignment to keep up the necessary order in the prison, guards did not get specific instructions about how to behave. The experiment was planned to have a two-week duration, but it had to be prematurely terminated after only six days because sadistic dynamics had emerged in and taken over the mock prison. Within days, the guards turned aggressive and abusive toward the prisoners and clearly enjoyed the cruel exercise of authority:

> What we saw was frightening. . . . The majority had indeed become prisoners or guards, no longer able to clearly differentiate between role playing and self. There were dramatic changes in virtually every aspect of their behavior, thinking and feeling. . . . Human values were suspended, self-concepts were challenged and the ugliest, most base, pathological side of human nature surfaced. (Zimbardo 1982, p. 249)

The implications of these experiments for ethical decision making in finance and investment are considerable because the results demonstrate the power *roles* can have over what a person perceives to be right and wrong and over what a person considers justified or even necessary (Brady and Logsdon 1988). Only a little imagination is required to infer from these studies that situational factors may also be decisive factors in (un)ethical investment decision making. For example, these results shed light on the collective practices of individuals in financial organizations that go against the law and violate fundamental professional rules (Daneke 1985). Examples of such practices in financial organizations abound—and not only in the recent history of the industry.

A case in point is the fraud committed by dozens of professionals during the Equity Funding Corporation of America scandal that occurred in 1973. Equity Funding sold funds and insurance policies to private consumers. Using an electronic program whose only purpose was to manage nonexistent insurance policies, almost 100 employees deceived investors and authorities alike in an organized scheme. Brady and Logsdon (1988) wrote that many of the employees were

> normal-average adults, not hardened criminals. The deviant organizational norms and the participants' organizational roles simply dominated their usual patterns of behavior as the conspiracy grew larger and more accepted. (p. 707)

A similar case of aggregate unethical behavior in the business world can be seen in the case of Beech-Nut Nutrition Corporation, which was at one time the second largest U.S. manufacturer of baby food. Employees of Beech-Nut collectively marketed and sold a chemical concentrate containing no apple juice whatsoever as "100% fruit juice" (Brief, Buttram, Dukerich, and Turner 2001; Welles 1988).

As these examples show, social influences go a long way toward explaining collectively unethical and evil behavior among students, investment professionals, and businesspeople.

Forms of Social Influence

In the workplace, social influence may take a variety of forms—offering information, attempting to persuade, suggesting a certain course of action, requesting a favor, ordering something, or demonstrating how something should be done (Kelman 2001). Social influence is ongoing in all areas of finance and investment professionals' work life—for example, in relationships between security analysts and potential clients as well as between analysts and the companies they cover.

Social influence plays a particularly important role in organizations where hierarchical structures usually establish marked power differences and asymmetrical relationships (as in most financial organizations). The context of organizational hierarchies gives rise to a broad spectrum of unethical strategies to influence others, ranging from coercion to ethically questionable "facilitation" tactics (Darley, Messick, and Tyler 2001). In the hierarchy of financial and investment organizations, it is legitimate for supervisors to influence their employees. For the influence to be ethical, however, clear boundaries must exist regarding the areas in which supervisors may influence subordinates and regarding the strategies that may be used to influence subordinates. Moreover, easily available mechanisms should be in place that can be activated if different opinions arise about what supervisors can expect subordinates to do and about whether power is being abused (Kelman 2001).

Strategies to influence others can be arranged along a continuum from little to much freedom of the person being influenced. These strategies range from coercion to manipulation to persuasion and, finally, to facilitation (Kelman and Warwick 1977).

1. *Coercion.* Coercion minimizes the freedom of the influenced finance professional. It is commonly expressed as a threat to deprive the other of something essential. For example, a supervisor announcing to his subordinate that he will make her professional life difficult and that her contract will not be renewed should she make public his sexual harassment is using coercion.

2. *Manipulation.* Manipulation can take a variety of forms. So-called environmental manipulation is a change in the alternatives available in the environment of the person being influenced. It leaves the other person a choice, but it simultaneously changes or reduces the alternatives available to the person. Manipulation can be seen in the case of a junior financial analyst whose report has determined that the return on investment in a company will be 12 percent. When his supervisor reads the report, he returns it to the analyst because no investment below a 25 percent return would be approved. The supervisor tells the analyst to "correct" the numbers after he does a new calculation (Badaracco and Webb 1995). Another example of environmental manipulation is the president of an investment firm who handpicks the members of a "retirement privileges committee" so that he can make sure the decision outcomes will benefit him personally (see Hoyt and Garrison 1997).

   So-called psychic manipulation limits the information made available to others and attempts to change their motivations. Consider the following example, in which a manager describes how her superior reacted after she had made him aware that he had forced her to use false numbers in a report. "He started treating other people better. He wasn't on my side anymore, and you needed him on your side to do things. He wasn't my buddy anymore . . . acting like you were not that smart anymore" (Badaracco and Webb 1995, p. 11).

3. *Persuasion.* In contrast to the heavy-handed tactics of coercion and manipulation, persuasion uses arguments and discussion to change the attitudes or behavior of another person. An example is an investment adviser persuading her customer to buy stocks of a technology company because of historically low price-to-earnings ratios in this sector and because the company may be taken over by another company.

4. *Facilitation.* Facilitation attempts to maximize freedom of choice of the influenced person by making resources and information available. For example, a supervisor facilitates the direction a subordinate is taking with his career by letting him work in various departments and gather impressions from experienced colleagues working in these departments.

This list of social influence strategies ranks the strategies from low to high ethical acceptability, albeit only in a general way. Higher values may in rare situations justify the use of coercion—for example, as in the case of a bank employee forcing customers out of the building to protect them from the danger of an armed robbery. In other situations, persuasion may serve unethical ends, as in the case of the supervisor at a financial firm persuading her new assistant that the routine of charging private dining expenses to a firm account will be in their common interest. Thus, the ethics of each strategy for influencing others ultimately depends on how the strategy is used in a particular situation (Kelman 2001).

The following account shows how influence tactics may be strategically planned to proceed unethically from persuasion to coercion:

> [T]hree steps are used in banking whether a banker is pitching a deal, executing a deal or attacking a colleague who's thinking of quitting. *Greed, Fear and Abandon.* Those are the three steps. First, persuade by talking about money and success. Stroke the ego and tell the clients what they want to hear. Act sincere. If this doesn't work, move to the second stage of the process—fear. Scare the shit out the clients and shake their confidence. Tell them that if they don't join the bank in a deal, then they will fail and be miserable. Finally, if this doesn't work the banker will abandon in an unusually rapid fashion. (Rolfe and Troob 2000, p. 261)

In this exaggerated sequence of social influence, all the tactics are being used to achieve a one-sided goal that does not take into consideration the welfare and interests of the person being influenced. The target in this scheme of social influence is being treated as an object, representing no more than a means to a desired end.

Ethical Impression Management

Whereas the previously discussed strategies aim at influencing others' behavior, *impression management* is at work when people aim to control the impressions others have of them. *Ethical* impression management is used to define actions and events for others in ways that shed an ethically favorable light on oneself (Schlenker 1980). It consists of self-presentation tactics that are used to paint one's actions and decisions as ethically sound (Payne and Giacalone 1990; Lawton 2006). A blatant example of such impression management was given earlier in the remark of former Enron Corporation Chief Executive Officer (CEO) Jeffrey Skilling: "We are the good guys. We are on the side of angels" (quoted in Jennings 2005, p. 51).

In the context of unethical decision making, impression management is particularly relevant when it is used to reframe ethically suspect behavior (Knouse and Giacalone 1992). All people—finance and investment professionals included—sometimes use such unethical means as lying, deceiving, or distorting the truth in their impression management. Indeed, the fact that impression management exists and that professionals know that others engage in it can lead to uncertainty about others' true ethical thinking and about the real meaning of their behavior.

Ethical impression management includes two kinds of tactics: reputation tactics and remedy tactics (Payne and Giacalone 1990).

1. *Reputation tactics.* When people use reputation tactics, they try to create a particular ethical image of themselves among others. They may engage in such strategies as association, ingratiation, or entitling. For example, they might try to *associate* themselves with other persons or outcomes that they know to be perceived as ethical. A CEO of an investment bank who mentions in a board meeting the good conversation he had with Warren Buffett at a charity dinner may be engaging in reputation tactics. Another reputation tactic is *ingratiation* (Jones 1964; Jones, Gergen, and Jones 1963). An example is flattering others and doing them favors in order to be liked by them and, consequently, to be judged as being ethical. Finally, an investment professional who uses *entitling* to develop a favorable ethical image of himself may claim credit for ethical successes by, for example, taking credit for the promotion decision that made a female colleague partner in an otherwise male-dominated investment firm.

2. *Remedy tactics.* These tactics are used to remove or improve unethical impressions others may have of someone after that person has done something unethical. If caught in unethical behavior, a person may engage in such verbal strategies as self-justification, excusing oneself, or apologizing. The difference between a justification and an excuse is the following: Although *self-justification* of behavior attempts to portray the behavior as legitimate (for example, "You have to understand my reasons for accepting the gift; they would have been insulted."), an *excuse* aims at minimizing the professional's personal responsibility for the behavior (for example, "Nobody explained to me exactly which expenses were company expenses and which were not"). When the circumstances of unethical behavior are so evident that they allow neither justification nor excuse, apologizing for the unethical action may be all that is possible. In *apologizing*, the financial professional caught in unethical behavior is at the mercy of others.

Not only individuals but also financial firms and institutions engage in ethical impression management for reputational and for remedial purposes. For example, firms make active use of impression management in order to influence public opinion after financial mismanagement, bribery, or unethical business practices (see Giacalone and Payne 1987). This behavior can be seen in computer firm Apple's handling of the controversy surrounding the company's practice of backdating stock options.[27] When Chief Executive Officer Steve Jobs, who had himself received a backdated grant, came under pressure, Apple used an excuse by claiming that he was aware of the backdating grants only "in a few instances," that he "did not . . . benefit from these grants," and that he "was unaware of the accounting implications." Simultaneously, Jobs issued a public apology for the problems and promised remedies "to ensure this never happens again" (Allison and Waters 2006, p. 30).

Fortunately, one might add ironically, specialized impression managers in the form of public relations professionals readily distribute "tips for turning down the heat" during such times of public ethical scrutiny (for examples of such advice, see Dittus 2007).

---

[27]In stock option backdating, prices of options (usually those issued to company employees or executives) are not set at their levels when they are granted but at levels of an earlier time when the price was lower. This ethically questionable practice is not illegal if it is disclosed to shareholders and authorities and properly accounted for.

8. Groups and Ethics

Finance and investment professionals do not ponder the ethics of their decisions and choose a course of action in a detached state of psychological isolation. Rather than thinking, feeling, and deciding merely as individuals, finance professionals are always members of groups, organizations, and the social collective formed by the investment community (Newcomb 1972; Oberlechner 2004b). This chapter focuses on a particularly important aspect of the dynamics of social influences on ethics—namely, the power of group membership and psychological group processes to create ethical and unethical behavior.

Conformity

Among all the psychological processes influencing the ethics of groups, *conformity* is the most basic and pervasive. Conformity is evident in all kinds of groups and in all kinds of decisions and behavior in which these groups engage. The beliefs, attitudes, decisions, and standards of people who interact with each other in a group have a tendency to converge, often until they are practically identical.

Thus, ethical conformity is the psychological process in which perceptions of the ethics of other group members become the basis for our own decisions and behavior. Group membership changes the attitudes and behavior of finance professionals in powerful ways. It leads individuals to orient their own ethical standards for behavior according to perceived, or suspected, norms of their work group (see Zeckhauser, Patel, and Hendricks 1991). Such a process, leading in this case to unethical conformity, was addressed by Warren Buffett after the scandal involving Salomon Brothers and U.S. Treasury auctions in the early 1990s (see Chapter 2). Buffett described the prevailing atmosphere at Salomon as "macho" and poignantly added, "I don't think the same thing would have happened in a monastery" (Hylton 1991, p. D1).

In a classic psychology experiment on conformity (Asch 1951, 1955), people were asked to make what seemed to be easy choices. They had to match the length of one original line to one of three comparison lines, which were of clearly different lengths. Each of the members of a group openly made, in their order of seating, an objective, straightforward choice. What one participant did not know was that all other persons in the group were actually confederates of the experimenter. These confederates had been secretly instructed to sometimes respond unanimously with a *wrong* judgment, and one after the other, they would declare that they perceived an obviously longer or obviously shorter comparison line to match the original line.

The responses of the other group members turned out to have a decisive effect on the perceptions and decisions of the actual participant in the experiment. Whereas comparison estimates in a control group were virtually without error, being exposed to the wrong judgments of others and having to declare publicly one's own opposing opinion dramatically increased the number of distorted estimates in the experimental group. Even participants who were strong enough to make dissenting judgments reported that they started to doubt their own eyes when other group members disagreed with them. Although the researchers found individual differences in how prone people were to giving in to group pressure (some participants never conformed to the wrong group judgment; others went with the majority nearly all the time), the findings clearly demonstrate how reluctant people are to express dissent with a perceived group consensus.

The tendency to conform in groups makes people change their public opinions even when there is a clearly contradicting, objective, physical reality (Peterson 2001). Of course, professionals confronted with ethical issues in the real-life world of finance and investment face more ambiguous demands than the clear-cut task of matching the length of lines. In ambiguous situations, however, conformity processes in groups also strongly influence the attitudes and the behavior of individual group members (Sherif 1936). Indeed, the psychological tendency to conform may be even stronger in unstructured decision tasks, where often no preformulated choices are available and where the line between what is right and what is wrong is blurred.

In financial and investment firms, ethical conformity appears in various connections between the ethical behavior of individuals and the influence of significant others and groups in the organization (Loe, Ferrell, and Mansfield 2000; O'Fallon and Butterfield 2005). Do these pressures to conform put into a hopeless situation those individual investment professionals who are ethical by themselves but become part of groups with less-than-ethical standards and norms? The answer provided by social psychology research is no. Indeed, much evidence gives hope for individuals resisting conformity when confronted with collective wrongdoing.[28] In specific situations, dissent by a single individual may exert a large influence on the unethical decision making in a group and dissent by small groups may influence organizational wrongdoing. This effect is more likely if the following conditions are met: The nonconformist is consistent. This person should not appear to be inflexible in a dogmatic way but should frame the dissent as something in line with existing social trends. Under these conditions, even if minority dissent is not able to force the majority to move in the right direction, it may lead majority representatives to reconsider questionable directives and to think about unrecognized ethical aspects of their behavior (Brief et al. 2001; Nemeth 1986).

---

[28]Baron and Byrne (1987); Berkowitz (1983); Brief et al. (2001); Moscovici (1985); Wolf (1985).

Ethical Group Shifts and Polarization

In the Sidney Lumet film *12 Angry Men*, 12 men in a jury room deliberate their verdict in the case of a young defendant in a (seemingly obvious) murder case. They are instructed by the judge that "in the event that you find the accused guilty, the bench will not entertain a recommendation for mercy. The death sentence is mandatory in this case." The discussion that follows among the jurors is a remarkable demonstration of the power of group processes on ethics—both the powerful influence of the group on the opinions and decisions of individuals and the powerful influence of an individual on the decisions of the group. When the jurors begin their deliberations, they are almost unanimous in their conviction that the defendant is guilty. Hours later, through the persistent influence of one juror (played by Henry Fonda), the group has switched to an undivided vote of not guilty. Although the film demonstrates that group processes influence ethical judgments, systematic knowledge of how psychological and social dynamics in groups operate helps us understand this influence (Brown 1986). These dynamics hold true also for groups operating in the finance and investment industry.

In addition to conformity, psychologists have observed that group interactions produce *risky shifts* and *group polarization* (Moscovici and Zavalloni 1969). The ethically potentially dangerous influence of these processes on the decision making of individuals was first described by Stoner (1961), who presented people in a study with "choice dilemmas" that involved a cautious and a risky alternative. The cautious alternative resulted in little but certain benefit; the risky course of action promised a large benefit but with only a small likelihood. When people were confronted with such dilemmas after they had participated in a group discussion that dramatically increased their tendency for risk taking, they experienced a risky-shift phenomenon. Psychologists soon realized that this shift toward increased willingness to take risks is a manifestation of group polarization—that is, the tendency in groups for *any* preference held by group members in the beginning to become more extreme during the course of group interaction (Moscovici and Zavalloni).

The implications of the phenomenon of group polarization for the ethics of group judgments are extremely important, as has been shown in the verdicts reached by juries (Bray and Noble 1978; Isozaki 1984). These group phenomena can also have a dramatic effect on the ethics of the decisions made by finance and investment professionals. When decisions result from group dynamics, they are likely to reflect systematically different ethics from the ethics that individuals alone would have displayed (Maital 1982). This phenomenon is most visible in psychological "groupthink."

Groupthink

Groupthink is a harmful, concurrence-seeking tendency of groups that is motivated by the members' conformity needs (Janis 1971). The implications of this "collective pattern of defensive avoidance" (Janis and Mann 1977, p. 129) go far beyond conformity, however, because groupthink leads the group members to become less realistic in their opinions, less efficient in using their intellectual resources, and less demanding in their moral standards (Plous 1993). Thus, a central aspect of the collective avoidance involved in groupthink concerns ethical considerations: Groupthink leads to unethical decision making by groups.

According to Irving Janis, the psychologist who identified this phenomenon, groupthink has eight symptoms, as shown in **Exhibit 2**. In other words, finance and investment professionals should be aware that when the ethical dynamics in a group that works closely together are weighed down by groupthink, the group members develop the false illusion that they are invulnerable. And the overconfidence embedded in this illusion may lead them to take excessive risks. Warnings are collectively discounted and rationalized away. Moreover, a misleading sense of unanimity in the group emerges from (1) group members who self-censor possible doubts or deviations from the seeming group consensus and (2) the pressure on group members who attempt to dissent from the consensus. Most importantly, group members develop an unquestioned belief in the group's own morality. This belief leads the group to ignore the ethical implications of the group's decisions, and it leads members to withhold from the group any information that could challenge the group's complacent certainty about the ethics of its decisions (Janis and Mann 1977).

Exhibit 2. The Eight Symptoms of Groupthink

1. An illusion of invulnerability, shared by most or all of the members, which creates excessive optimism and encourages taking extreme risks.
2. Collective efforts to rationalize in order to discount warnings which might lead the members to reconsider their assumptions before they recommit themselves to their past policy decisions
3. An unquestioned belief in the group's inherent morality, inclining the members to ignore the ethical or moral consequences of their decisions.
4. Stereotyped views of rivals and enemies as too evil to warrant genuine attempts to negotiate, or as too weak or stupid to counter whatever risky attempts are made to defeat their purposes.
5. Direct pressure on any member who expresses strong arguments against any of the group's stereotypes, illusions, or commitments, making clear that such dissent is contrary to what is expected of all loyal members.
6. Self-censorship of deviations from the apparent group consensus, reflecting each member's inclination to minimize to himself the importance of his doubts and counterarguments.
7. A shared illusion of unanimity, partly resulting from this self-censorship and augmented by the false assumption that silence implies consent.
8. The emergence of self-appointed "mindguards"—members who protect the group from adverse information that might shatter their shared complacency about the effectiveness and morality of their decisions.

Source: Janis and Mann (1977, p. 130f).

Examples abound of how groupthink influences the ethics of decisions made by groups of finance and investment professionals. The dangerous dynamics of groupthink were involved in such events as the Salomon Brothers Treasury auction scandal and the collectively practiced "check kiting" at the brokerage firm E.F. Hutton. The unethical and risky nature of these practices would be obvious to any individual investor; a law degree or a PhD in finance is not required to realize the wrong involved in auction bidding that clearly violates a Treasury rule and in deliberately writing checks that will bounce. In the case of Hutton, having been influenced by groupthink, managers developed a skillful scheme in which money managers knowingly wrote uncovered checks on bank accounts. These checks then were deposited into other bank accounts where Hutton immediately began to earn interest. The managers counted on the fact that either the simultaneous overdraft would go unnoticed for a short while or that the bank would not complain because of Hutton's importance as one of the leading brokers in the nation. In this way, Hutton's managers were able to accumulate US$250 million in "free loans" day by day (Sims 1992). This example illustrates that the harmful consequences of groupthink in groups of finance professionals are real and that their damage can be assessed in hard currency.

9. Power, Leadership, and Ethics

Like all organizations, the firms operating in the investment world have explicit and implicit rules that distribute power and authority among their members. These rules define the relationships among the members of the organization. For example, they define whether certain relationships are hierarchical or nonhierarchical. In addition, these rules shape the professionals' access to information and other resources and prescribe the behavior alternatives available to them. For instance, because novice employees lack important resources, contacts, and knowledge, they are often in a position of dependence on others and rarely in a position to exercise power in the company.

Arrangements of power and authority are much more than value-free structures defining the nature of work relationships in investment organizations. Access to power and the use of authority also affect ethics. Although the ethical dimension in the decisions and actions of the professionals in financial organizations is determined by power dynamics on all hierarchical levels, leaders play a particularly important role because they convey organizational values to all members of the firm and set the ethical climate (Grojean, Resick, Dickson, and Smith 2004).

This chapter examines the consequences of power for ethics in investment organizations, the sources of power, and the requirements of ethical leadership. When some people see ethical (or legal) borders being crossed by organizational leaders, these people may become whistle blowers.

Power and Ethics

To finance and investment professionals, having power means that they are able to make others do what they want in the way they want it done and when they want it done. Power and the uneven distribution of power is an inherent characteristic of hierarchical organizations. Depending on its source and its extent, power can have a significant impact on ethics in the organization and even on an industry as a whole.

Whether they are aware of it or not, professionals use their power to extend their ethics (or lack of ethics) to other members of the organization. A professional's ability to influence other members of the organization rests on five types of power: reward, coercive, legitimate, referent, and expert (French and Raven 1996).

- *Reward power.* Perhaps the most obvious type of power, reward power is based on a person's capacity to provide positive incentives. For example, those who determine the size of a firm's year-end bonuses hold reward power over those who receive the bonuses.

- *Coercive power.* This type of power rests on the person's capacity to penalize others. In contrast to the power to determine the size of bonuses is the coercive power of a supervisor warning her sales team that she will fire those who fail to meet their sales quotas. Excessive coercive pressure to meet certain financial goals is often a warning sign of ethical collapse (Jennings 2006b).
- *Legitimate power.* Legitimate power is exercised by those members of firms whom others believe are entitled to power and have the right to demand certain behavior. The authority of those with legitimate power is recognized and accepted by others in the organization. The basis for legitimate power is provided by relationship structures in the firm (French and Raven 1996). For example, a senior analyst telling his assistant to conduct the company research needed to prepare a report is making use of his legitimate power. Differences (often culturally based) in assistants' perceptions of a supervisors' legitimate power may lead to differences in the willingness of subordinates to accept the orders of a senior analyst.
- *Referent power.* Power that comes to a person or an organization from others' feelings of identification or membership with the person or organization is referent power. This type of power contributed to the collapse of Enron Corporation. Based on their loyalty and emotional attachment to the company, Enron employees hesitated to inform others of the unethical actions of their supervisors (Cohan 2002).
- *Expert power.* Expert power depends on others' perception that a person has knowledge and expertise. For example, today, a demand for ecologically safe investments—"green" funds—is on the rise. Specialists in this area of investing will thus gain power in their organizations from their expert knowledge.

Usually, a combination of types of power gives someone power over other members of an organization and allows them to influence the behavior of others in an ethics-relevant way. Unfortunately, the more power an individual has, the more temptation the individual may feel to use that power unethically (Kipnis 1976). Compounding that problem is the fact that questioning or even challenging the ethics of persons in high-power positions often has negative repercussions for professionals in lower positions of power. Repercussions range from being left out of the dissemination of important information given to one's colleagues to demotion to loss of one's job.

The ethical use of power in financial organizations starts with leaders and managers who exercise their power over others in an ethically responsible way.

Ethical Leadership

Leaders play a central role in establishing an ethical organizational culture (Grojean et al. 2004; Verschoor 2006). They do so in formal ways (for example, by formulating official codes of ethics) and in informal ways (for example, by acting as a role model or by the ethics implicit in their decisions) (Trevino and Nelson 2007).

Unethical or ethically neutral leadership—as in a leader's failure to set ethical standards or a leader's focus that is too narrowly confined to profits—facilitates an unethical business culture. The leadership at Salomon Brothers before the bond-trading scandal in the early 1990s (see Chapter 2) clearly demonstrates this phenomenon. Before this scandal broke, the goals established by the company's leadership were guided purely by profits. The organizational culture that emerged from this leadership did little to support and foster ethical decision making by its members; ethics was seen as a barrier to earnings. This approach resulted in unethical and illegal conduct by company employees (Sims 2000).

Unfortunately, the list of charismatic but ultimately unethical leaders in the corporate finance world is long. It includes such prominent actors as WorldCom's Scott Sullivan, Tyco International's Mark Swartz, and Enron's Andrew Fastow. What is particularly remarkable and ironic is that these leaders at some point in their careers were awarded the title "CFO of the Year" by *CFO* magazine (Jennings 2005). Thus, the following questions arise: What distinguishes purely charismatic and fascinating leaders from leaders who are also ethical? What do ethical leaders do to foster ethics in their organizations?

Although there is certainly no recipe for ethical leadership, answers can be found on two levels: (1) the things leaders do to exercise their power ethically within the company and (2) the things leaders do to function as ethical role models.

- *Exercising power ethically.* One of the characteristics of ethical leaders in organizations manifests itself in how they exercise their own power and authority over their subordinates. They promote not only their personal vision but are careful to integrate their subordinates' visions into the goals of the organization. Rather than one-sidedly advocating top-down messages, they actively encourage open communication and are open to critiques from which they can learn. In other words, ethical leaders try to serve others rather than first and foremost promoting their own personal gain (Howell and Avolio 1992).

- *Representing an ethical role model.* Ethical leaders take their function of being ethical role models very seriously. In fact, they know that they are the central role models in establishing and running an ethical organization. Unlike their unethical counterparts, ethical leaders are committed to high ethical standards and apply such standards to everyone within the company. When ethical issues arise within the company, leaders do not hesitate to approach the issues and respond to them without unnecessary delay. Ethical leaders take a proactive stance on ethical problems. Former U.S. President Richard Nixon admitted to failure on exactly this count in the 1972 Watergate scandal that led to his resignation:

    > [W]hile I was not involved in the decision to conduct the break-in, I should have set a higher standard for the conduct of the people who participated in my campaign and Administration. I should have made such actions unthinkable. I did not. (Duffield and McCuen 2000, p. 79; see also Nixon 1990)

Ethical leaders gather information about the legal and ethical considerations of their business and see ethical standards as a primary measure of performance, often with customer and public welfare rather than the company's welfare as the guideline. To ethical leaders, the lower standards of other companies do not serve as an excuse for ethical compromises (Sims and Brinkman 2002).

These two dimensions of ethical leadership have also been used to define the "moral manager" and "moral person" dimensions of ethical leadership. As a moral manager, an ethical leader conveys clear expectations for the ethical conduct of others and holds them responsible for their ethical conduct. As a moral person, an ethical leader serves as a personal role model by demonstrating such individual characteristics as integrity, honesty, and fairness (Trevino and Nelson 2007).

To summarize, leaders play a decisive role in shaping the ethics of any organization, including finance and investment organizations. The ethical leader sets a personal example and conveys and reinforces ethical standards by an ethical exercise of power (Sims and Brinkman 2002).

Whistle Blowing

When the standards of ethical leadership are violated and leaders engage in unethical actions, a possible and highly visible outcome is employees' whistle blowing. Whistle blowers are organization members who, usually because they feel powerless, release information and evidence of illegal or unethical conduct in the organization to parties who are able to take action (Boatright 2007; Greenberger, Miceli, and Cohen 1987).

Definitions of what exactly constitutes whistle blowing in firms vary. Sometimes, whistle blowing is perceived as an act of informing by organization members to outside people or entities. In such cases, it may be characterized as dissent, public accusation, and disloyalty to the organization (Jubb 1999). Others see whistle blowing more broadly, including not only disclosures via channels outside the organization but also complaints made through internal channels. In practice, internal whistle blowing and external whistle blowing are closely linked. Many times, the use of internal channels is the first step. If the organization ignores this information, the whistle blower proceeds to channels outside the organization (Near and Miceli 1996).

At times, whistle blowers appear to be simply disappointed employees. They may be disgruntled and angry because they believe they have been treated unfairly—not being promoted, for example. They may want to enrich themselves or draw attention away from their own weaknesses. Often, however, whistle blowers sacrifice their jobs to speak out loud about and stop what they believe is unethical, illegal, or dangerous. Then, they become what Grant (2002, p. 391) called "saints of secular culture." Three such saints were even named "Persons of the Year" in 2002 by *Time* magazine—Sherron Watkins of Enron, Cynthia Cooper of WorldCom, and Coleen Rowley of the U.S. Federal Bureau of Investigations (Lacayo and Ripley 2002).

The fact that these three public whistle blowers are women may not be a coincidence; female students have been shown to be less tolerant of ethically questionable behavior than male students (Cagle and Baucus 2006), and women in general are more ready than men to perceive specific professional practices as unethical (Franke, Crown, and Spake 1997). Some analyses of whistle blowers show that women are less likely, however, to blow the whistle externally (Sims and Keenan 1998). Age, tenure, and a high position within the company increase the likelihood of an employee blowing the whistle (Mesmer-Magnus and Viswesvaran 2005). Finally, there are not only personal but also cultural factors that influence the likelihood of whistle blowing. For example, in one study, the tendency to speak up against major wrongdoing was found to be stronger among managers from the United States than among managers from Croatia (Tavakoli, Keenan, and Cranjak-Karanovic 2003).

Whistle blowing can result in extremely harmful consequences to the whistle blower and to the company involved. Employees who blow the whistle may be confronted with retaliation inside the organization—from losing valuable personal and professional support to losing their jobs. For organizations, whistle blowing can result in a damaged image, questions from worried customers, enquiries by legal authorities, and public scandals that shatter the organization (as was the case for the accounting firm Arthur Andersen) or even an entire industry (as the financial industry was rocked by the savings and loan scandal of the 1980s). When a whistle blower goes public, the decades required to build a good reputation for a financial institution may be wiped out in the seconds it takes to write a newspaper headline.

Thus, not only is it the ethical responsibility of institutions to provide employees with effective internal means for righting wrongs, but it is also in the self-interest of the organizations. To be effective, mechanisms should exist for employees to react quickly to wrong and illegal behavior within the organization (especially by those higher than the employee in power and authority) and report it without fear of retaliation. Only organizational structures that support speaking up against ethical wrongdoing can counteract the damage resulting from the ethical violations of leaders and superiors.

Organizational measures that help ensure that concerns and complaints regarding ethics can be addressed appropriately are presented in the following chapter.

10. Organizational Culture and Ethics

From the corruption at Enron Corporation and WorldCom in North America to the fraud at BAWAG Bank in Europe to bribery at the Hong Kong Stock Exchange, violations of ethics and the law in the finance and investment industry can be observed around the globe (Crawford and Mollenkamp 1991). However, whereas ethical issues and a concern for ethics are universal, how ethics is perceived and managed by investment professionals in different nations is affected by cultural differences.

The importance of culture to ethics can be seen in, for example, the cultural dimension called "power distance" (the basic relationship of individuals to authorities). The lower that power distance is in a culture, the less fearful employees are of their superiors and the more democratic and consultative decision making is preferred to an authoritarian, top-down style (Hofstede 1991). Because power distance is greater in the Pacific Rim nations (Hong Kong, Japan, Singapore, and Thailand) than in the United States or Canada, finance professionals in the former countries show a greater willingness to follow ethical standards set by authorities, and they experience codes of conduct as greater deterrents to unethical behavior than do finance professionals in North America (Baker and Veit 1998). Cultural values also affect how much weight finance professionals assign in their decision making to the interests of external stakeholders and how loyal they feel toward their organizations and work groups (Jackson 2001).

In addition to differences in values among national cultures, differences in organizational cultures also influence the ethics of the professionals working in this industry. The organizational ethical culture is expressed in the ethical norms and beliefs that are shared within an organization by the members of the organization (Key 1999).

As has been shown in the repeated and seemingly endless cycle of ethics scandals followed by tighter regulations by authorities followed by ethics scandals (Jennings 2003), laws and regulations by themselves are inadequate for upholding ethical behavior in the world of finance and investments. Culture, in contrast, has a significant impact on the ethics-related perceptions and the behavior of finance professionals (Sims and Gegez 2004).

Establishing and maintaining an ethically nurturing organization lead to a series of positive outcomes. Studies show that an organizational culture that takes ethics seriously increases organizational commitment and improves the fit between people and the organization. An ethical culture also enhances employees' workplace experience (Valentine, Godkin, and Lucero 2002). Moreover, an organizational culture that emphasizes the importance of ethics, that rewards ethical behavior, and that provides ethics training leads to better moral judgments by employees (Bowen 2004). Thus, to be ethical as individuals, professionals in the finance and investment industry require organizations that are equally committed to ethics; they require finance and investment companies that reinforce and nurture ethical behavior.

But what can finance and investment firms that are facing the tension between profit seeking and ethical behavior do to instill a culture of ethics? This chapter explains how the ethics in an investment organization's culture can be evaluated and describes the support structures that can be used to implement an organizational culture of ethics.

Assessing Organizational Ethical Culture

To instill a culture of ethics, organizations are well advised to start by conducting a full examination of their current ethical culture. This can be achieved by, for example, surveys that ask employees about their level of agreement with observations such as "In this organization, people are encouraged to take full responsibility for their actions," "Ethical behavior is the norm in this organization," "Unethical behavior is punished in this organization," "Top managers of this organization are models of ethical behavior," and "Organizational rules and procedures regarding ethical behavior serve only to maintain the organization's public image" (Key 1999; Trevino, Butterfield, and McCabe 1995).

The answers to these and other ethics-related questions will allow a comprehensive assessment of the current ethical culture in an investment firm. This assessment will not only identify specific areas of ethical concern; it will also allow informed predictions about the ethical element in employees' professional behavior. For example, when the culture in an organization is always reminding employees of efficiency and profitability and never of ethical concerns, employees will perceive that their only goal is profit maximization and will act accordingly. When the organizational culture shows genuine commitment and respect for ethical standards, employees will be motivated to maintain those standards (Bartlett and Preston 2000).

Supporting Organizational Ethical Culture

Once the prevailing ethical culture in an investment firm has been assessed, a number of organizational structures can be put in place to support the firm and its employees in maintaining and improving an ethical organizational culture. These support structures include codes of conduct, ethics officers, and ethics committees.

Codes of Conduct. Codes of conduct, if prepared, reviewed, and used correctly, can greatly support financial and investment firms that are striving for a culture of ethics. Such codes are written documents that function as formal organizational guidelines for corporate and individual behavior.[29] They define ethics-related expectations, both of the company and of individual employees.

Codes of conduct influence employees' perceptions of how ethically their company operates (Valentine and Barnett 2002). Moreover, these codes influence the work climate positively, resulting in more ethical behavior and an increase in the moral awareness of employees (VanSandt, Shepard, and Zappe 2006). Codes of conduct are important from the beginning of the relationship between a financial firm and its employees: Employees who are introduced to the firm's code of conduct during orientation perceive ethics and incorruptibility as more important to the organization than do others (Valentine and Johnson 2005).

Codes of conduct are not always effective in supporting a culture of ethics in the organization. A poorly designed code of conduct—that is, a lengthy and highly abstract formal document—may do nothing more than get dusty on the shelves of the legal department. Few employees will be aware of the contents of such a code and of the ethical issues discussed therein (Bartlett and Preston 2000). To enhance the effectiveness of a code of conduct, the following steps can be taken during the creation, implementation, and administration of it (Martens and Day 1999; Schwartz 2004):

- Have employees play an active role in establishing the code.
- Involve the senior management actively in establishing and promoting the code.
- Allow concerns about the code to be addressed early in the process of establishing the code.
- Include specific examples that make explicit both desired and negative behaviors in the code. For example, vague terms, such as "social responsibility," should instead be defined in terms of expected behavior or what actions should be avoided completely (Gray 1990).
- Ensure that the code avoids a one-sided adoption of nationally biased values. For example, an international bank headquartered in New York City should avoid narrowly promoting U.S.-centric values.
- Define a mechanism for enforcing the code that is easily available to all.
- Assure that the contents of the code of conduct are reviewed and updated periodically (Valentine and Johnson 2005).

Ethics Officers and Ombudspersons. A culture of ethics in financial and investment organizations can also be promoted and supported through the work of ethics officers and ombudspersons. Ethics officers can help establish an ethical climate in firms through the development of activities and programs (McDonald 2000). To work effectively, ethics officers should be independent (to be credible and to deal with unethical behavior professionally) and have insider status (to have

---

[29]The CFA Institute Centre for Financial Market Integrity has made available the Asset Manager Code of Professional Conduct since 2005 (www.cfapubs.org/loi/ccb).

easy access to employees and important communications). To effectively deal with specific ethical problems arising in a firm, they need to have sound knowledge of the firm's culture and rules and of ethics theory (Izraeli and BarNir 1998).

Ombudspersons usually offer themselves as impartial third-party mediators to resolve conflicts in an atmosphere of confidentiality (Dunfee and Werhane 1997).

Although installing ethics officers and ombudspersons has become popular in recent years, these people and the work they do require substantial support from the organization's management to amount to more than just organizational window dressing. As one expert dryly remarked:

> If [the chief ethics officer] is really good and works closely with top management, they could make a difference. . . . Equally, they could make no difference at all, if the commitment from top management isn't there. (Clark 2006)

Ethics Committees. Ethics committees can be especially helpful in promoting a culture of ethics in organizations. The basic functions of these committees are to develop a corporate code of conduct, review and update ethics policies (including the code of conduct), supervise ethics-related activities, formulate a policy for a specific ethics-related issue, answer questions about corporate ethics, and respond to employee complaints (Brytting 1997). Once a committee has been established, managers and other employees may present their concerns to the committee, which then follows through (McDonald 2000). Membership in ethics committees may rotate to give all employees the chance to participate in the active shaping of the company's ethical culture and to prevent a handful of people from monopolizing this function.

Unfortunately, ethics committees are probably still uncommon in business life, including at financial and investment firms. A survey conducted among New Zealand firms in 2003 found that fewer than 10 percent of the companies had an ethics committee (Pajo and McGhee 2003).

Improving Support Structures. At present, a trend is growing for building up ethics support structures, especially among U.S. businesses. Yet, ethics scandals continue to occur. How can the impact of such organizational support structures as codes of conduct, ethics officers, and ethics committees be made truly effective?

One way to improve the effectiveness and practicability of ethics support may be to combine the structures (McDonald 2000). These structures can be effective, however, only if the firm's senior management shows (not merely espouses) a genuine commitment to an organizational culture of ethics. Finally, firms aiming at strengthening the organization's culture of ethics should bear in mind three key elements. First, they should carefully establish a balanced psychological contract between the employer and the employee. This psychological agreement should focus on reciprocity, by which both employer end employee give and receive in ethics-relevant ways. In other words, there are not only ethical requirements of the employee but there is also an organization that actively encourages and supports ethical behavior. Second, the firm should not only create but should also constantly improve its ethical organizational culture. Third, the firm should strengthen employees' commitment to the organization through, for example, increasing the visibility of ethically superior work within the organization (Sims 1991).

11. Compensation and Reward Systems

In the culture of investment organizations and in the relationships between these organizations and their employees, compensation and reward systems form a fundamental ingredient. In fact, compensation systems are among the most relevant determinants of ethical behavior within organizations. Although managerial thinking about compensation and rewards usually centers on such issues as motivation and fairness, these systems are also a direct reflection of organizational ethics and of underlying organizational values that may contradict the values that are openly espoused by the organization.

Fairness of Compensation

For a long time, compensation was viewed exclusively as a market transaction. This traditional economic perspective is best captured by the motto "a fair day's wage for a fair day's work." According to this perspective, the main concern of managers and organizations in designing compensation systems is to ensure that the systems fairly and accurately reflect the economic worth that workers contribute to the company (Bloom 2004).

Many financial institutions violate this basic economic requirement of compensation systems, however, as the following example shows:

> Twice a year all the DLJ [Donaldson Lufkin & Jenrette] associates piled into a conference room. . . . They read the names of the analysts off one by one in alphabetical order. As each name was read, the associates who had worked with that analyst weighed in with their judgment of the analyst's worth. Those assessments were used in turn to determine the analysts' bonuses—bonuses that ranged anywhere from $30,000 for a first-year analyst to $100,000 for a third year analyst. . . .
>
> There were two problems with these review sessions. The first was that outside of the review sessions we'd been conditioned to always toe the party line. Independent thought was not valued. We were processors. We weren't allowed to have our own opinions; we were only allowed to have our managing directors' opinions. . . . The other problem with the analyst review sessions was that they inevitably degenerated into outlets for the months of frustration that we ourselves had suffered at the hands of our vice presidents, senior vice presidents and managing directors. . . . If our rite of passage was going to be difficult, we were surely going to make the analysts' rite of passage that more miserable. . . .

> As we sat in these reviews, there was an unspoken concern in the back of our minds. . . . We knew that the reviews didn't do a good job rewarding the analysts who deserved to be rewarded and canning the ones who didn't. . . . we also knew that a roomful of vice presidents, senior vice presidents and managing directors were reviewing us the same way we were reviewing the analysts. (Rolfe and Troob 2000, p. 228f)

This example also shows that to employees of financial firms, the psychological meaning of fairness goes well beyond economic aspects; it incorporates such issues as trust, relationships, and ethics.

Although monetary fairness remains a critical component of ethical compensation systems, financial organizations need to supplement the economic focus on distributive justice (represented by the magnitude of allocated payments) with fairness considerations of a more psychological nature—that is, *procedural fairness* and *interactional fairness*.

Procedural fairness addresses the way compensation is allocated. The term refers to employees' perception that the process used to determine and distribute compensation is fair. Procedural fairness is violated when, for example, employees can see that the process is inconsistent and biased (Bloom 2004), as in the DLJ example: "We knew that the reviews didn't do a good job rewarding the analysts who deserved to be rewarded and canning the ones who didn't."

Interactional fairness addresses how employees feel they are treated by other people, particularly those who make compensation decisions and execute compensation decisions (Bloom 2004). Interactional fairness is also violated in the DLJ example, as shown by the associates' experience of "months of frustration that we ourselves had suffered at the hands of our vice presidents, senior vice presidents and managing directors."

Organizations and managers in the finance and investment industry would be well advised not to overemphasize monetary compensation at the expense of other motivators. Overreliance on monetary rewards encourages employees to operate at low stages of moral reasoning (see Chapter 3). In the first two stages of moral reasoning, individuals define right and wrong simply in relation to external punishments and rewards and they may even manipulate others in their search for rewards. Thus, if the organization focuses on monetary compensation in its relationship with employees, it may contribute to unethical behavior over the long term (Baucus and Beck-Dudley 2005). In other words, compensation systems reflect organizational values and have a powerful influence on the behavior of investment professionals—especially on the ethics of their behavior (Bloom 2004).

Unintended Consequences of Compensation and Reward Systems

The ethical aspects of compensation systems are particularly evident in brokerage, where payments to practitioners at a firm are frequently in the form of commissions. Commissions were originally introduced as a better way to motivate employees than plain salaries. Take salespersons, for example. The more customers a salesperson persuades and the more financial products the customers purchase, the higher the firm's revenue and, with commissions, the higher the compensation of the salesperson. In this sense, compensation systems based on commissions align the interests of the agent (the salesperson) and the principal (the firm) within an agency relationship.

In the investment industry, agency relationships are usually more complex, however, than one agent working on behalf of one principal. The agent (the salesperson) is working on behalf of not one but two principals—the firm and the client. Such triangular patterns create difficult issues in investment management just as they do in other kinds of human relationships. Although commissions can help protect the interest of one of the principals, they may undermine the interest of the other, as the following example shows:

> In January, 1988, the phones were quiet. After the blood bath just months before, investors were afraid to step back into the market. It was my third month as a full-fledged, series 7-licensed, straight-commissioned broker. I was 26, single and poor. My rent was due, my ego hungry. My firm had a new product for me. The closed-end bond fund. A neat idea. I could earn 4 cents on the dollar. . . .
>
> I got on the phone and started calling current clients and cold calling prospective ones. "I have this new product. Are you interested?"
>
> "It's a conservative investment." I told them. My company had told me so.
>
> "And you don't pay any commission because it's a new issue," I added.
>
> I sold quite a bit—although not enough to earn me a trip to Hawaii. And clients seemed happy—until 3 months later.
>
> Clients did not pay commissions on new issues. That was true. What I did not tell them, though, was that the fund borrowed money to cover the expenses. For several months after the fund started trading, my company would support the stock in the open market. After this initial support, the stock could be expected to drop 7 percent—3 percent reflecting the underwriting fee and 4 percent representing my commission. (Kurland 1999, pp. 29–30)

This example vividly illustrates that one of the major ethical questions in the investment industry is to what extent commissions influence ethical behavior and create unethical outcomes (Duska 1999). In a wide range of situations involving financial professionals, the individual's reward has become an end in itself, not a means to an end. Customers have vague feelings that their brokers are more interested in closing deals than in their financial well-being. Brokers stoop to such illegal practices as churning—buying and selling stocks excessively only to generate large commission fees. Thus, the commission in a badly designed reward system can be detrimental to ethics in a financial organization.

One of the greatest ethical dangers that financial organizations create for their members is the inconsistent foolishness of hoping for certain ethical behavior and outcomes while *de facto* rewarding completely different behavior and outcomes. Far too often, organizations reward unwanted behaviors and actively discourage ethical behavior by their monetary motivation (Kerr 1975). Take, for example, an investment firm that in its code of ethics encourages its employees to act in the best interest of clients but, at the same time, has established and forcefully practices a straight-commission compensation system that is solely based on quantitative outcomes. Kurland (1991) described such a situation in which an initiative of some employees to explicitly reward the espoused value (acting in the best interest of clients) gets no support from the investment firm's top management.

Such inconsistency between the compensation system and the ethical values espoused by the firm creates an organizational environment of ethical ambivalence. Investment professionals working for this firm, in regard to the ethics of their own behavior, will feel like they are being pulled in psychologically opposite directions. Their ethical ambivalence expresses the (unintended) consequences of a badly designed compensation system, and this ambivalence will often lead to unethical choices.

Similar unintended unethical consequences can be observed in an evolution in compensation that has taken place at the top of financial and investment firms. At the beginning of this process, corporate chief executive officers (CEOs) felt pressure to switch to paying for performance and to having more of their own earnings at risk—that is, to be connected to the firm's performance. The next step of the process introduced stock options for CEOs and the promise of shares tied to stock price and other measures of performance. Unethical leadership started when the CEOs realized that to get the maximum return from their salary and options, they needed their firm's stock price to go up substantially. When they could not accomplish this goal by building their companies ethically, they were tempted to resort to ethically questionable actions and strategies. In this way, through the so-called law of unintended consequences, an initially good intention became distorted and ultimately produced highly unethical results.[30]

In addition to official compensation and reward systems, implicit reward systems shape the (un)ethical behavior of professionals. Implicit rewards can be found in, for example, the promotion processes. The questions of who is favored by the supervisor, who gets promoted, and with what kind of ethical track record are critical because those who are favored and promoted are the models shaping the

---

[30] From Marshall Carter, personal communication, 27 September 2005.

behavior of other employees. Frequently, the influence of implicit reward systems on ethics in investment organizations goes unnoticed. These systems can be discovered, however, by examining what kinds of management reactions do *not* take place in an organization. This aspect is nicely illustrated by Sherlock Holmes explaining the "curious incident" that led him to solve the case in Arthur Conan Doyle's short story "Silver Blaze." Holmes finds the clue he needs in the dog that did *not* bark on the night of the murder, which indicated that the dog knew the intruder. "That was the curious incident!" Hidden organizational reward systems may surface in unethical behavior that is *not* punished by the organization. To feel that you are treated fairly and to trust that the workplace is just, members of an organization must see that violations of ethical standards have consequences and that violators are disciplined. If these reactions do not take place, the message is that unethical behavior is tolerated, even implicitly rewarded, by the organization (Trevino and Ball 1992; Trevino and Nelson 2007).

Financial and investment firms that genuinely care about the ethical conduct of employees need to be aware of the impact of their compensation and reward systems. They need to design and implement systems that are "ethically enabling," not "ethically disabling" (Jansen and Von Glinow 1985). The leaders and managers of organizations should regularly monitor the systems for fairness and for unintended consequences for the ethics of employees. For these leaders, a valuable lesson is to be learned from the work of therapists with children who are considered "problem children." Therapists have found that these children do what is rewarded. Employees also do what is rewarded, and leaders should be conscious of the fact that the nature of the rewards may not always be explicit (Trevino and Nelson 2007).

12. Ethics Training

Formal instruction in ethics for finance and investment professionals is not a new idea. As early as the 19th century, ethics was a part of business education, but decades later, during the 1980s, in the aftermath of the insider-trading scandals, business schools painfully rediscovered that educating ethically responsible leaders was vital (McWilliams and Nahavandi 2006). Corporations of all kinds also recognized the need for better ethics training for their employees. This renewed recognition of the importance of ethics training is reflected in an extensive survey conducted during that period. Out of 1,000 large U.S. companies that were asked to cite important areas for future corporate training, a clear majority listed ethics training (Saari, Johnson, McLaughlin, and Zimmerle 1988).

In the 1990s, legislation in the United States boosted corporate education and the introduction of ethical standards and compliance programs. Since 1991, the U.S. Sentencing Guidelines have provided incentives for companies to establish measures to guard against legal violations (LeClair and Ferrell 2000). In 1996, U.S. companies spent an estimated US$1 billion on ethics training (Khalfani 1996).

Lengthy ethical guidelines have had little impact, however, on preventing new corporate scandals. Rather, in the first years of the new millennium, alarming misdeeds at financial firms and other companies put ethics in the spotlight once again. The demise of such leading companies as Arthur Andersen, Enron Corporation, and WorldCom is still fresh in the minds of investors and the general public. Again, financial and investment companies are trying to address the issue by developing codes of conduct and by introducing ethics training programs.

Doubts about the efficacy of these measures, however, abound. As a recent poll conducted among finance executives shows, more than half of the chief financial officers who were questioned thought that at least a 50–50 chance exists of a fraudulent act on a scale similar to the Enron debacle occurring in the next decade (Durfee 2006). Such gloomy predictions by practitioners in the field clearly indicate the need for a fundamental ethical change in the financial and investment industry. Part of the necessary change would be a new commitment from these organizations to educating and training their members and leaders in ethical issues.

Clearly, the relationship between ethics and the business practices of financial institutions is complex in this profit-focused industry in which most workers have considered ethical behavior to be a constraint. A balance between profits and ethics can only be achieved if professionals in the finance and investment industry learn to see ethics as a value and a goal (Dobson 1997).

Previous chapters have shown the importance of leadership and organizational culture for developing such a perspective on ethics. This chapter shows how ethics in a firm can be strengthened through education and training that allows employees to understand the individual and social dynamics of (un)ethical behavior and helps them become ethically mature. The chapter reviews the efforts of organizations inside and outside the finance and investment industry to teach ethics. It describes the characteristics of successful ethics programs, the methods used in these programs, and their effectiveness and limitations.

Characteristics of Successful Ethics Training

To be effective, ethics training and education programs should identify the program goals and focus on specific learning outcomes for program participants (Ritter 2006; Sims and Felton 2006). But what kinds of goals and outcomes are realistic for a professional training program in ethics? What kinds of seminar objectives lead to results, and which programs are efficient?

The following psychological and educational insights can assist financial leaders and managers in answering these questions. Sound ethics training and education programs should:

- *Increase finance professionals' awareness of actual ethical issues.* Rather than teaching abstract principles of morality, ethics training programs in the finance and investment industry should focus on raising participants' awareness of possible ethical issues in real-life professional situations. In a globalized professional world and a constantly changing business environment, finance professionals may often face new situations, and the ethical components involved in these situations may not always be obvious (Sims and Felton 2006). It is important, therefore, for participants to understand that reflection about ethics is not limited to predefined course topics. Awareness of ethics and dealing with ethical aspects are continuing endeavors throughout one's career; they do not stop at the end of the classroom sessions.
- *Provide participants with practical frameworks.* Ethics training should not only provide participants with theoretical knowledge but also help them develop practical ethics problem-solving skills. This aspect is important not only for managers but for all employees (Knouse and Giacalone 1997). The goal of this part of successful ethics training is to provide employees with a hands-on conceptual framework that supports ethics in the professional decisions that employees face every day (McDonald 2000).

A simple example of such a practical framework is a "decision tree" that helps decision makers steer a course through ethics-relevant business decisions. The decision tree starts with the question of whether a planned action is legal; only if it is legal may the decision maker proceed to the next step. Here, the question is whether the action maximizes shareholder value. If it does, then the decision maker proceeds to Step 3, where the question is whether the behavior is also ethical. If the decision maker answers at Step 2 that the action does *not* maximize shareholder value, the decision maker is asked whether it would be unethical to *not* take the action. If so, the leader is advised to proceed with the action and to simultaneously inform shareholders of its effect (Bagley 2003).

- *Create a climate conducive to learning.* To ensure that the ethics training provides a meaningful learning experience, the learning environment must allow participants to feel comfortable about expressing their opinions and concerns (McWilliams and Nahavandi 2006). A core aspect of such a learning environment is a climate of open discussion and reciprocity that is based on giving and receiving by all participants and that is not merely about the trainer's or supervisor's contributions. Education research shows that training programs for adult learners should leave room for input and choice as well as provide opportunities for discussion and reflection on personal experience (LeClair and Ferrell 2000).

  Thus, ethics courses should focus on creating an interactive climate that actively encourages participation. Experience-based learning approaches that provide real-life applications are especially appealing to participants and effective (Sims and Felton 2006).

  Live instruction is an important component of a climate conducive to learning. Face-to-face discussions in small-class settings stimulate participants' sensitivity. The focus of these discussions should be on active decision making rather than on passive lectures (Ponemon and Felo 1996).

- *Focus on concrete, relevant issues.* To be perceived as relevant and to encourage meaningful discussion among finance and investment practitioners, ethics training programs should focus on problems specific to the investment industry, not on general principles of business ethics. Material that covers realistic scenarios relevant to the finance industry (for example, insider trading, fraud, breach of fiduciary duty) and to the specific organization is most effective (Knouse and Giacalone 1997). Participants should, for example, be asked to determine key areas of ethical issues in their work and decide which underlying ethical principles should govern the handling of these issues.

- *Establish clear links to the firm's ethical guidelines and codes of conduct.* The discussion of concrete issues should be integrated with and should spell out links to relevant documents and regulations established by the participant's firm, such as existing ethics guidelines and a corporate code of conduct. In this way, established ethical guidelines are likely to be understood and can actually be implemented by employees on a daily basis. Often, this aspect of ethics training is considered particularly relevant by participants: Linking the training contents to the firm's ethical guidelines and codes of conduct satisfies finance professionals' desire to make ethical guidelines applicable (LeClair and Ferrell 2000).

- *Include a follow-up to the training sessions.* Follow-up sessions deepen the learning process that is initiated in the training sessions, no matter which training approach is used. Follow-up programs (and allowing some time to elapse between training and the follow-up program) allow employees the possibility of digesting and refreshing what they learned in the initial training (Knouse and Giacalone 1997). Many approaches to such a follow-up after the training sessions are possible. Firms may, for example, circulate newsletters to draw attention to key ethical messages, discuss postseminar case studies, highlight the behavior of ethical employees, and/or establish work groups or networking circles (Ponemon and Felo 1996).

Although all of these facets are important ingredients of successful ethics training programs, the programs cannot work without authentic support from firms' top management. For ethics programs to be effective, the following organizational preconditions need to be met. First, the firm's senior managers need to send clear messages about their full support of the training program and about an ethical vision for the firm. Second, the top management needs to ensure that the firm's code of conduct is written in an understandable and concrete manner, rather than being written in abstract legal language. Third, the code must include a statement of specific commitment of the organization to the ethical behavior of its employees (McDonald 2000; Ponemon and Felo 1996). Not even the best ethics training program can work if real commitment to a culture of ethics is missing among the firm's leaders.

Training Methods

Finance and investment firms that wish to provide ethics education for their employees face a wide spectrum of available training programs and educational methods. Contemporary possibilities range from on-site training to distance learning and involve participation in philosophical lectures and experiential simulations. The following paragraphs discuss some of the possibilities.

- *Philosophical approaches.* The discussion of philosophical approaches to ethics is a possible starting point for ethics training. Philosophical ideas may help individuals in the financial industry understand and analyze ethical problems as they arise in people's daily work and serve as a first basis for codes of conduct and ethical guidelines. A purely normative or philosophical approach to ethics training misses out, however, on factors that are of crucial importance in the work of investment professionals. For example, this approach fails to pay adequate attention to the corporate and social surroundings in which investment professionals operate (Brady and Logsdon 1988).
- *Case study.* Cases studies are commonly used in business ethics training programs. Research on finance students' ethical perceptions before and after case studies were presented to and discussed by the students supports the effectiveness of this method (Cagle and Baucus 2006). A traditional case study approach,

however, may easily result in a purely academic, and thus insulated, discussion that neglects aspects that are critical to real-life ethical behavior of investment professionals. In other words, case discussions run the danger of preparing participants only for abstract ethical decision making, not for concrete ethical behavior. Moreover, investment professionals should be able to act ethically not only in specific scenarios but also in many different settings and situations (Brady and Logsdon 1988). Finally, although case studies help raise awareness of the complexity of ethical dilemmas and improve analytical skills (McWilliams and Nahavandi 2006), they may not promote engagement and emotional involvement on the part of program participants.

- *Critical Incident Technique.* The Critical Incident Technique requires more active involvement from participants than do philosophical approaches and traditional case studies. This technique aims at facilitating effective ethical decision making in highly relevant areas of professional behavior. For this technique, employees familiar with a problem area (for example, with churning or unauthorized trading) are asked to identify what is ethical behavior and what is unethical behavior for a professional facing specific situations that may arise in this area (Dean 1992).

  The Critical Incident Technique encourages independent thinking and invites participants to distinguish between average ethics on the job and outstanding ethical behavior in ethics-relevant areas. It involves participants in identifying such areas, in formulating specific situations that may arise, and in defining outstanding ethical performance. In doing so, the Critical Incident Technique ensures authentic observations and highly specific solutions.

- *Game-based and simulation methods.* Such companies as Lockheed Martin and Sony have developed game-based ethics programs.

  In an early game-based approach at Citicorp, small teams of employees were presented with a sequence of ethical dilemmas related to conflicts of interest, sexual harassment, reporting ethical concerns, and confidentiality issues. The teams discussed these issues and selected one action from among four predefined action alternatives. After the teams had presented their solutions, their answers were discussed, often heatedly, by all seminar participants and were scored according to scales predetermined by the company's senior managers. The senior managers were also present at the seminar to explain their reasons and expectations, to react to appeals from the teams, and even to change a game's score if the team presented convincing solutions (Trevino and Nelson 2007). This approach facilitates teamwork and cooperation; it also provides timely feedback to participants. Most importantly, such games are stimulating and encourage active engagement with ethical issues (LeClair and Ferrell 2000).

Another interactive ethics training approach is represented by simulation programs. In the simulations, participants familiarize themselves with the character of specific roles they take on and with the values and goals of simulated organizations. Simulation programs can allow a high degree of interaction among the participants and can function as a practice stage in ethical decision making in workplace situations (LeClair and Ferrell 2000).

Effectiveness of Ethics Training Programs

Corporate ethics training programs provide encouraging results in terms of their impact and effectiveness. In fact, employees in organizations offering ethics training programs have a more positive perception of their organization's ethical culture than do employees in other organizations (Valentine and Fleischman 2004). Moreover, a survey that has been distributed for decades among graduates of Columbia Business School shows that ethics education programs encourage ethical behavior. Specifically, individuals who had encountered ethics training were less likely to engage in unethical actions (Delaney and Sockell 1992).

Naturally, not all methods of ethics training are equally successful. Many textbooks cover ethics in insufficient depth (Baetz and Sharp 2004). Lectures and self-study alone are unlikely to make a difference in how finance professionals understand and approach ethical issues (Izzo, Langford, and Vitell 2006). Other passive forms of learning, such as listening to lectures and watching videotapes, also do not have a great impact on the ethics of decisions and behavior. Only interactive and personally engaging methods will lead to tangible outcomes among participants (LeClair and Ferrell 2000).

The most effective ethics training programs are well thought out and embedded in the context of the organization. To create long-term effects, finance and investment firms need to thoroughly plan and implement ethics training programs. The most frequent mistakes made by organizations are failure to set clear and reasonable goals for the program, lack of support for the program from senior management, and unsuitability of the program for average employees because, for example, the code of conduct is written in purely legal language (Martens and Day 1999).

To conclude, ethics training may not be able to turn morally corrupt individuals into saintly finance and investment professionals, but effective ethics education raises awareness of ethical concerns in investment professionals. Moreover, it improves ethical decision making by increasing professionals' skill and comfort in addressing ethical issues. Acquiring sound psychological knowledge about the ethical interplay of personal, situational, and organizational factors and developing and implementing a genuine ethical commitment by the organization offer investment professionals a solid basis for this new comfort with ethical dimensions of their work.

13. Conclusion

> The line separating good and evil passes through every human heart.
> —Aleksandr Solzhenitsyn
> *The Gulag Archipelago*

Buffeted by the latest scandals in their industry, individuals and firms in the finance and investment profession sometimes wonder whether their efforts to instill ethics are worthwhile. In this monograph, I have tried to show that these efforts can be effective if they are based on sound psychological principles.

Understanding the psychology of ethics is important because this discipline reveals to us the *dynamics* involved in ethical decision making—not only on the part of individuals, as addressed by the quotation from Russian writer Aleksandr Solzhenitsyn, but also in groups and organizations. This knowledge allows us to understand why some investment professionals behave ethically and others violate ethical (and, perhaps, legal) standards. This knowledge warns us of situational and social forces that result in otherwise ethical persons committing clearly unethical deeds. And this knowledge points us in the right direction for managing the ethical conduct of ourselves, our colleagues, and our subordinates.

Professionals working in the finance and investment industry are often in situations where they must decide whether to engage in ethical or unethical behavior. And they are vulnerable to the temptation to act unethically because of the large sums of money at stake, the size of the industry and the markets versus their own anonymity as "worker bees," and their training as economically "rational" strivers after maximum profits (and, perhaps, their lack of any training in ethics).

The psychological view on what motivates people to be ethical offers insights into those and other vulnerabilities and introduces the concept of self-actualizing individuals who are motivated by more than money. They want to live a decent life and carry out good work. They want to be ethical.

The philosophical approaches to ethical decision making propose ideals of how people should behave and form a good starting point for our understanding and for training programs. But the goal is to implement the ideals. This monograph has explored how people make real-life ethical decisions through a series of steps. People are not likely to skip from Step 1 (awareness) immediately to Step 4 (action). So, time and practice are needed for ethical decision making. And although ethics training may not be able to turn morally corrupt individuals into saintly professionals, effective ethics education can raise awareness of ethical concerns and stimulate practice in ethical decision making.

Along the way, hindering our progress, are the implicit and unconscious biases that we all carry around. We see ourselves as ethical, and we rationalize our behavior when we do not act ethically. We may believe that we can do no wrong, so what others call manipulation is just persuasion. Or we may tell ourselves that we have no power at all, so we are not at fault. We tend to make snap judgments. We may think we are impervious to the group's thinking, but psychological studies have shown that most of us are not—that we need to belong and be accepted by others. Peer pressure and conformity to perceived authority is alive and well among grown-ups. Awareness of these psychological barriers to ethical action can help us overcome them.

Psychology also sheds light on how individuals become the role models, for good or ill, in their organizations, families, and society. The ethical leader can be identified by actions—the ethical exercise of power—and by modeling what it is to be ethical. Psychology suggests how the ethical leader became that way through a series of stages in moral development. Knowing the stages of maturity and how these stages affect the ethics of decisions, we can see where people are along the continuum from self-centered greed to self-actualization by their actions and statements. Reaching ethical maturity is the goal. The ethically mature individuals are the people we want in charge. And if we are leaders, that is the stage we want to reach.

References

Abdolmohammadi, M., and J. Sultan. 2002. "Ethical Reasoning and the Use of Insider Information in Stock Trading." *Journal of Business Ethics*, vol. 37, no. 2: 165–173.

Allison, K., and Waters, R. 2006. "Apple Investors Shrug Off Fears on Jobs Apology." *Financial Times* (6 October):30.

Andrews, K.R. 1989. "Ethics in Practice." *Harvard Business Review*, vol. 67, no. 5: 99–104.

Argyris, C., R. Putnam, and D.M. Smith. 1985. *Action Science*. San Francisco: Jossey-Bass.

Asch, S.E. 1951. "Effects of Group Pressure upon the Modification and Distortion of Judgments." In *Groups, Leadership, and Men*. Edited by H. Guetzkow. Pittsburgh: Carnegie Press.

———. 1955. "Opinions and Social Pressure." *Scientific American*, vol. 193, no. 5: 31–35.

Ashkanasy, N.M., C.A. Windsor, and L.K. Trevino. 2006. "Bad Apples in Bad Barrels Revisited: Cognitive Moral Development, Just World Beliefs, Rewards, and Ethical Decision-Making." *Business Ethics Quarterly*, vol. 16, no. 4:449–473.

Bacon, K.H., and K.G. Salwen. 1991. "Summer of Financial Scandals Raises Questions about the Ability of Regulators to Police Markets." *Wall Street Journal* (28 August):A10.

Badaracco, J.L. 1998. "The Discipline of Building Character." *Harvard Business Review*, vol. 76, no. 2:115–124.

Badaracco, J.L., and A.P. Webb. 1995. "Business Ethics: A View from the Trenches." *California Management Review*, vol. 37, no. 2:8–28.

Baetz, M.C., and D.J. Sharp. 2004. "Integrating Ethics Content into the Core Business Curriculum: Do Core Teaching Materials Do the Job?" *Journal of Business Ethics*, vol. 51, no. 1:53–62.

Bagley, C.E. 2003. "The Ethical Leader's Decision Tree." *Harvard Business Review*, vol. 81, no. 2: (February)18–19.

References

Baker, H.K., and E.T. Veit. 1998. "A Comparison of Ethics of Investment Professionals: North America versus Pacific Rim Nations." *Journal of Business Ethics*, vol. 17, no. 8:917–937.

Banaji, M.R., M.H. Bazerman, and D. Chugh. 2003. "How (Un)ethical Are You?" *Harvard Business Review*, vol. 81, no. 12:56–64.

Bandura, A. 1988. "Mechanisms of Moral Disengagement." In *Origins of Terrorism: Psychologies, Ideologies, Theologies, State of Mind*. Edited by W. Reich. New York: Cambridge University Press.

Bandura, A., C. Barbaranelli, G.V. Caprara, and C. Pastorelli. 1996. "Mechanisms of Moral Disengagement in the Exercise of Moral Agency." *Journal of Personality and Social Psychology*, vol. 71, no. 2:364–374.

Barber, B.M., R. Lehavy, M. McNichols, and B. Trueman. 2006. "Buys, Holds, and Sells: The Distribution of Investment Banks' Stock Ratings and the Implications for the Profitability of Analysts' Recommendations." *Journal of Accounting and Economics*, vol. 41, nos. 1–2:87–117.

Baron, R.A., and D. Byrne. 1987. *Social Psychology: Understanding Human Interaction*. 5th ed. Boston: Allyn and Bacon.

Bartlett, A., and D. Preston. 2000. "Can Ethical Behaviour Really Exist in Business?" *Journal of Business Ethics*, vol. 23, no. 2:199–209.

Baucus, M.S., and C.L. Beck-Dudley. 2005. "Designing Ethical Organizations: Avoiding the Long-Term Negative Effects of Rewards and Punishments." *Journal of Business Ethics*, vol. 56, no. 4:355–370.

Berger, K.S., and R.A. Thompson. 1995. *The Developing Person through Childhood and Adolescence*. 4th ed. New York: Worth.

Berkowitz, L. 1983. "Imitation, Conformity, and Compliance." In *Psychological Foundations of Organizational Behavior*. Edited by B.M. Staw. Oakland, NJ: Scott, Foresman.

Bernstein, W.J. 2006. "Corporate Finance and Original Sin." *Financial Analysts Journal*, vol. 62, no. 3 (May/June):20–23.

Bethwaite, J., and P. Tompkinson. 1996. "The Ultimatum Game and Non-Selfish Utility Functions." *Journal of Economic Psychology*, vol. 17, no. 2:259–271.

Beu, D.S., and M.R. Buckley. 2004. "This Is War: How the Politically Astute Achieve Crimes of Obedience through the Use of Moral Disengagement." *Leadership Quarterly*, vol. 15, no. 4:551–568.

Bloom, M. 2004. "The Ethics of Compensation Systems." *Journal of Business Ethics*, vol. 52, no. 2:149–152.

Boatright, J.R. 2007. *Ethics and the Conduct of Business*. 5th ed. Upper Saddle River, NJ: Pearson Prentice Hall.

Bonvin, J.M., and P.H. Dembinski. 2002. "Ethical Issues in Financial Activities." *Journal of Business Ethics*, vol. 37, no. 2:187–192.

Bowen, S. 2004. "Organizational Factors Encouraging Ethical Decision Making: An Exploration into the Case of an Exemplar." *Journal of Business Ethics*, vol. 52, no. 4:311–324.

Brady, F.N., and J.M. Logsdon. 1988. "Zimbardo's 'Stanford Prison Experiment' and the Relevance of Social Psychology for Teaching Business Ethics." *Journal of Business Ethics*, vol. 7, no. 9:703–710.

Bray, R.M., and A.M. Noble. 1978. "Authoritarianism and Decisions of Mock Juries: Evidence of Jury Bias and Group Polarization." *Journal of Personality and Social Psychology*, vol. 36, no. 12:1424–1430.

Brief, A.P., R.T. Buttram, J.M. Dukerich, and M.E. Turner. 2001. "Collective Corruption in the Corporate World: Toward a Process Model." In *Groups at Work: Theory and Research*. Edited by M.E. Turner. Mahwah, NJ: Lawrence Erlbaum Associates.

Brown, R. 1986. *Social Psychology*. 2nd ed. New York: Free Press.

Brytting, T. 1997. "Moral Support Structures in Private Industry—The Swedish Case." *Journal of Business Ethics*, vol. 16, no. 7:663–697.

Caccese, M.S. 1997. "Ethics and the Financial Analyst." *Financial Analysts Journal*, vol. 53, no. 1 (January/February):9–14.

Cagle, J.A.B., and M.S. Baucus. 2006. "Case Studies of Ethics Scandals: Effects on Ethical Perceptions of Finance Students." *Journal of Business Ethics*, vol. 64, no. 3:213–229.

CFA Institute. 2005. "Code of Ethics and Standards of Professional Conduct" (www.cfainstitute.org/centre/ethics/code/pdf/english_code.pdf; retrieved 4 March 2007).

———. 2007. "Our Mission, Vision, and Strategic Objectives" (www.cfainstitute.org/aboutus/overview/mission.html; retrieved 25 February 2007).

Christie, R., and F.L. Geis. 1970. *Studies in Machiavellianism*. New York: Academic Press.

Clark, H. 2006. "Chief Ethics Officers: Who Needs Them?" (www.forbes.com/leadership/2006/10/23/leadership-ethics-hp-lead-govern-cx_hc_1023ethics.html; retrieved 25 February 2007).

"Cleaning Up Salomon's Mess." 1991. *New York Times* (22 August):A26.

Cohan, J.A. 2002. "'I Didn't Know' and 'I Was Only Doing My Job': Has Corporate Governance Careened Out of Control? A Case Study of Enron's Information Myopia." *Journal of Business Ethics*, vol. 40, no. 3:275–299.

Colby, A., and L. Kohlberg. 1987. *The Measurement of Moral Judgment, Vol. 1: Theoretical Foundations and Research Validation; Vol. 2: Standard Issue Scoring Manual*. Cambridge, U.K.: Cambridge University Press.

Colby, A., K. Lawrence, J. Gibbs, and M. Lieberman. 1994. "A Longitudinal Study of Moral Judgment." In *New Research in Moral Development*. Edited by B. Puka. New York: Garland Publishing.

Corcoran, K.J., and J.B. Rotter. 1987. "Morality-Conscience Guilt Scale as a Predictor of Ethical Behavior in a Cheating Situation among College Females." *Journal of General Psychology*, vol. 114, no. 2:117–123.

Crain, W.C. 1985. *Theories of Development: Concepts and Application*. 2nd ed. Englewood Cliffs, NJ: Prentice-Hall.

Crane, A., and D. Matten. 2004. *Business Ethics: A European Perspective*. Oxford, U.K.: Oxford University Press.

Crawford, D., and C. Mollenkamp. 1991. "Hong Kong Exchange Ex-Chairman Pleads Guilty to More Charges." *Wall Street Journal* (15 July):A8.

Daneke, G.A. 1985. "Regulation and the Sociopathic Firm." *Academy of Management Review*, vol. 10, no. 1:15–20.

Darley, J.M. 2001. "The Dynamics of Authority Influence in Organizations and the Unintended Action Consequences." In *Social Influences on Ethical Behavior in Organizations*. Edited by J.M. Darley and D.M. Messick. Mahwah, NJ: Lawrence Erlbaum Associates.

Darley, J.M., D.M. Messick, and T.R. Tyler. 2001. *Social Influences on Ethical Behavior in Organizations.* Mahwah, NJ: Lawrence Erlbaum Associates.

Dean, P.J. 1992. "Making Codes of Ethics 'Real.'" *Journal of Business Ethics*, vol. 11, no. 4:285–290.

Delaney, J.T., and D. Sockell. 1992. "Do Company Ethics Training Programs Make a Difference? An Empirical Analysis." *Journal of Business Ethics*, vol. 11, no. 9:719–727.

de Mott, D.K.D. 2001. "Ethics." *Gale Encyclopedia of Psychology* (http://www.findarticles.com/p/articles/mi_g2699/is_0004/ai_2699000457/print; retrieved 2 April 2005).

Department of Justice. 2003. "Eight Former Employees of Defunct Brokerage Firm Hampton Porter Investment Bankers Are Indicted by Federal Grand Jury." U.S. Department of Justice (http://www.usdoj.gov/opa/pr/2003/June/03_crm_370.htm; retrieved 25 February 2007).

Diamond, M.A., and G.B. Adams. 1999. "The Psychodynamics of Ethical Behavior in Organizations." *American Behavioral Scientist*, vol. 43, no. 2:245–263.

Dienhart, J., D. Moberg, and R. Duska, eds. 2001. *The Next Phase of Business Ethics: Integrating Psychology and Ethics.* Oxford, U.K.: Elsevier Science/JAI Press.

Dittus, G. 2007. "Tip Sheet: Successfully Managing a Public Investigation: Four Tips for Turning Down the Heat." *PR News*, vol. 63, no. 20 (May 21).

Dobson, J. 1993. "The Role of Ethics in Finance." *Financial Analysts Journal*, vol. 49, no. 6 (November/December):57–61.

———. 1997. "Ethics in Finance II." *Financial Analysts Journal*, vol. 53, no. 1 (January/February):15–25.

———. 2005. "Monkey Business: A Neo-Darwinist Approach to Ethics Codes." *Financial Analysts Journal*, vol. 61, no. 3 (May/June):59–64.

Donaldson, W.H. 2003. Testimony Concerning Global Research Analyst Settlement before the Senate Committee on Banking, Housing and Urban Affairs (7 May): http://www.sec.gov/news/testimony/ts050703whd.htm.

Dreman, D. 1995. "Outpsyching the Market—1995 Money Guide." *Forbes* (19 June):162–168.

Duchon, D., D. Ashmos, and K.J. Dunegan. 1991. "Avoid Decision-Making Disaster by Considering Psychological Bias." *Review of Business*, vols. 1–2, no. 13:13–18.

Duffield, J.F., and R.H. McCuen. 2000. "Ethical Maturity and Successful Leadership." *Journal of Professional Issues in Engineering Education and Practice*, vol. 126, no. 2:79–82.

Dunfee, T.W. 2001. "Marketlike Morality Within Organizations." In *Social Influences on Ethical Behavior in Organizations*. Edited by J.M. Darley and D.M. Messick. Mahwah, NJ: Lawrence Erlbaum Associates.

Dunfee, T.W., and P. Werhane. 1997. "Report on Business Ethics in North America." *Journal of Business Ethics*, vol. 16, no. 14:1589.

Durfee, D. 2006. "Enron: End of an Era." *CFO*, vol. 22, no. 8:20.

Duska, R. 1999. "The Ethics of Reward Systems in the Financial Services Industry." *Business and Society Review*, vol. 104, no. 1:34–41.

———. 2005. "Ethics in Financial Services." In *Perspectives in Business Ethics*. 3rd ed. Edited by L.P. Hartmann. Boston: McGraw Hill.

Eichenwald, K. 1991. "Salomon Reduces Bonuses by $110 Million." *New York Times* (30 October):D1.

———. 2005. *Conspiracy of Fools*. New York: Random House Broadway.

Elm, D.R., and M.L. Nichols. 1993. "An Investigation of the Moral Reasoning of Managers." *Journal of Business Ethics*, vol. 12, no. 11:817–833.

Fang, M.L. 2006. "Evaluating Ethical Decision-Making of Individual Employees in Organizations—An Integration Framework." *Journal of American Academy of Business*, vol. 8, no. 2:105–112.

Fazio, R.H. 1986. "How Do Attitudes Guide Behavior?" In *Handbook of Motivation and Cognition: Foundations of Social Behavior*. Edited by R.M. Sorrentino and E.T. Higgins. New York: Guilford Press.

Fazio, R.H., and T. Towles-Schwen. 1999. "The MODE Model of Attitude-Behavior Processes." In *Dual-Process Theories in Social Psychology*. Edited by S. Chaiken and Y. Trope. New York: Guilford Press.

Festinger, L. 1957. *A Theory of Cognitive Dissonance*. Stanford, CA: Stanford University Press.

Ford, R.C., and W.D. Richardson. 1994. "Ethical Decision Making: A Review of the Empirical Literature." *Journal of Business Ethics*, vol. 13, no. 3:205–221.

Forte, A. 2005. "Locus of Control and the Moral Reasoning of Managers." *Journal of Business Ethics*, vol. 58, nos. 1–3:65–77.

Franke, G.R., D.F. Crown, and D.F. Spake. 1997. "Gender Differences in Ethical Perceptions of Business Practices: A Social Role Theory Perspective." *Journal of Applied Psychology*, vol. 82, no. 6:920–934.

French, J.R.P., and B. Raven. 1996. "The Bases of Social Power." In *Classical Readings in Organizational Behavior*. 2nd ed. Edited by J.S. Ott. Belmont, CA: Wadsworth.

Frey, B.F. 2000. "The Impact of Moral Intensity on Decision Making in a Business Context." *Journal of Business Ethics*, vol. 26, no. 3:181–195.

Gaudine, A., and L. Thorne. 2001. "Emotion and Ethical Decision-Making in Organizations." *Journal of Business Ethics*, vol. 31, no. 2:175–187.

Gerrig, R.J., and P.G. Zimbardo. 2005. *Psychology and Life*. 17th ed. Boston: Allyn and Bacon.

Giacalone, R.A., and S.L. Payne. 1987. "Are Business Leaders Staging a Morality Play?" *Business and Society Review*, vol. 62 (Summer):22–26.

Gibson, J.T., M. Haritos-Fatouros, S. Milgram, and B.J. Bushman. 1991. "Conformity and Obedience." In *Readings in Social Psychology: General, Classic, and Contemporary Selections*. Edited by W.A. Lesko. Boston: Allyn and Bacon.

Gigerenzer, G., and P.M. Todd. 1999. *Simple Heuristics That Make Us Smart*. Oxford, U.K.: Oxford University Press.

Grant, C. 2002. "Whistle Blowers: Saints of Secular Culture." *Journal of Business Ethics*, vol. 39, no. 4:391–399.

Gray, R.H. 1990. "Business Ethics and Organisational Change." *Leadership and Organization Development Journal*, vol. 11, no. 3:12–21.

Greenberger, D.B., M.P. Miceli, and D.J. Cohen. 1987. "Oppositionists and Group Norms: The Reciprocal Influence of Whistle-Blowers and Co-Workers." *Journal of Business Ethics*, vol. 6, no. 7:527–542.

Grojean, M.W., C.J. Resick, M.W. Dickson, and D.B. Smith. 2004. "Leaders, Values, and Organizational Climate: Examining Leadership Strategies for Establishing an Organizational Climate Regarding Ethics." *Journal of Business Ethics*, vol. 55, no. 3:223–241.

References

Güth, W., H. Kliemt, and A. Ockenfels. 2003. "Fairness versus Efficiency: An Experimental Study of (Mutual) Gift Giving." *Journal of Economic Behavior and Organization*, vol. 50, no. 4:465–475.

Güth, W., and R. Tietz. 1990. "Ultimatum Bargaining Behavior: A Survey and Comparison of Experimental Results." *Journal of Economic Psychology*, vol. 11, no. 3:417–449.

Hagstrom, R.G. 2005. *The Warren Buffett Way*. 2nd ed. Hoboken, NJ: John Wiley and Sons.

Haney, C., C. Banks, and P. Zimbardo. 1973. "Interpersonal Dynamics in a Simulated Prison." *International Journal of Criminology and Penology*, vol. 1, no. 1:69–97.

Hansell, S. 1994. "Kidder Reports Fraud and Ousts a Top Trader." *New York Times* (18 April):A1.

Hartikainen, O., and S. Torstila. 2004. "Job-Related Ethical Judgment in the Finance Profession." *Journal of Applied Finance*, vol. 14, no. 1:62–76.

Hoaglund, J. 1984. "Ethical Theory and Practice: Is There a Gap?" *Journal of Business Ethics*, vol. 3, no. 3:201–205.

Hofstede, G. 1991. *Cultures and Organizations: Software of the Mind*. New York: McGraw-Hill.

Hogarth, R.M. 1981. "Beyond Discrete Biases: Functional and Dysfunctional Aspects of Judgmental Heuristics." *Psychological Bulletin*, vol. 90, no. 2:197–217.

Howell, J.M., and B.J. Avolio. 1992. "The Ethics of Charismatic Leadership: Submission or Liberation?" *The Executive*, vol. 6, no. 2:43–54.

Hoyt, P.D., and J.A. Garrison. 1997. "Political Manipulation within the Small Group: Foreign Policy Advisers in the Carter Administration." In *Beyond Groupthink: Political Group Dynamics and Foreign Policy-Making*. Edited by P. 't Hart, E.K. Stern, and B. Sundelius. Ann Arbor: University of Michigan Press.

Hylton, R.D. 1991. "Salomon's Remaining Challenges." *New York Times* (19 August):D1.

Isozaki, M. 1984. "The Effect of Discussion on Polarization of Judgments." *The Japanese Psychological Research*, vol. 26, no. 4:187–193.

Izraeli, D., and A. BarNir. 1998. "Promoting Ethics through Ethics Officers: A Proposed Profile and an Application." *Journal of Business Ethics*, vol. 17, no. 11: 1189–1196.

Izzo, G.M., B.E. Langford, and S. Vitell. 2006. "Investigating the Efficacy of Interactive Ethics Education: A Difference in Pedagogical Emphasis." *Journal of Marketing Theory and Practice*, vol. 14, no. 3:239–248.

Jackson, T. 2001. "Cultural Values and Management Ethics: A 10-Nation Study." *Human Relations*, vol. 54, no. 10:1267–1302.

James, H. 2001. *The Deutsche Bank and the Nazi Economic War against the Jews*. Cambridge, U.K.: Cambridge University Press.

Janis, I.L. 1971. "Groupthink." *Psychology Today*, vol. 43 (November):44, 46, 74–76.

Janis, I.L., and L. Mann. 1977. *Decision-Making: A Psychological Analysis of Conflict, Choice, and Commitment*. New York: The Free Press.

Jansen, E., and M.A. von Glinow. 1985. "Ethical Ambivalence and Organizational Reward Systems." *Academy of Management Review*, vol. 10, no. 4:814–822.

Jennings, M.M. 1998. "Ethics: Why It Matters and How You Do It." *The Government Accountants Journal*, vol. 47, no. 4:11–22.

———. 2003. "The Critical Role of Ethics." *The Internal Auditor*, vol. 60, no. 6:46–51.

———. 2005. "Ethics and Investment Management: True Reform." *Financial Analysts Journal*, vol. 61, no. 3 (May/June):45–58.

———. 2006a. *Business Ethics: Case Studies and Selected Readings*. 5th ed. Mason, OH: Thomson.

———. 2006b. "The Seven Signs of Ethical Collapse." *European Business Forum*, vol. 25 (Summer):32–38.

Johnson, M. 1993. *Moral Imagination: Implications of Cognitive Science for Ethics*. Chicago: University of Chicago Press.

Johnson, R.C., M.J. Ackerman, and H. Frank. 1968. "Resistance to Temptation, Guilt Following Yielding, and Psychopathology." *Journal of Consulting and Clinical Psychology*, vol. 32, no. 2:169–175.

Jolley, J.M., and M.L. Mitchell. 1996. *Lifespan Development: A Topical Approach*. Madison, NJ: Brown and Benchmark.

Jones, E.E. 1964. *Ingratiation*. New York: Appleton-Century-Crofts.

Jones, E.E., K.J. Gergen, and R.E. Jones. 1963. "Tactics of Ingratiation among Leaders and Subordinates in a Status Hierarchy." *Psychological Monographs*, vol. 77, no. 3:20.

Jones, J., D.W. Massey, and L. Thorne. 2003. "Auditors' Ethical Reasoning: Insights from Past Research and Implications for the Future." *Journal of Accounting Literature*, vol. 22, no. 3:45–103.

Jones, T.M. 1991. "Ethical Decision Making by Individuals in Organizations: An Issue-Contingent Model." *Academy of Management Review*, vol. 16, no. 2:366–395.

Jubb, P.B. 1999. "Whistleblowing: A Restrictive Definition and Interpretation." *Journal of Business Ethics*, vol. 21, no. 1:77.

Kegan, R. 1982. *The Evolving Self: Problem and Process in Human Development*. Cambridge, MA: Harvard University Press.

Kelemen, M., and T. Peltonen. 2001. "Ethics, Morality and the Subject: The Contribution of Zygmunt Bauman and Michel Foucault to 'Postmodern' Business Ethics." *Scandinavian Journal of Management*, vol. 17, no. 2:151–166.

Kelman, H.C. 2001. "Ethical Limits on the Use of Influence in Hierarchical Relationships." In *Social Influences on Ethical Behavior in Organizations*. Edited by J.M. Darley and D.M. Messick. Mahwah, NJ: Lawrence Erlbaum Associates.

Kelman, H.C., and D.P. Warwick. 1977. "The Ethics of Social Intervention: Goals, Means, and Consequences." In *The Ethics of Social Intervention*. Edited by G. Bermant, H.C. Kelman, and D.P. Warwick. Washington, DC: Hemisphere.

Kerr, S. 1975. "On the Folly of Rewarding A, While Hoping for B." *Academy of Management Journal*, vol. 18, no. 4:769–783.

Key, S. 1999. "Organizational Ethical Culture: Real or Imagined?" *Journal of Business Ethics*, vol. 20, no. 3:217–225.

Khalfani, L. 1996. "As Employers Focus on Ethics Training, Cottage Industry for Consultants Grows." *Wall Street Journal* (12 August):B4B.

Kidder, R.M. 1995. *How Good People Make Tough Choices: Resolving the Dilemmas of Ethical Living*. New York: HarperCollins.

Kipnis, D. 1976. *The Powerholders*. Chicago: University of Chicago Press.

Knouse, S.B., and R.A. Giacalone. 1992. "Ethical Decision-Making in Business: Behavioral Issues and Concerns." *Journal of Business Ethics*, vol. 11, nos. 5–6:369–377.

———. 1997. "The Six Components of Successful Ethics Training." *Business and Society Review*, vol. 98:10–13.

Kohlberg, L., and R.H. Hersh. 1977. "Moral Development: A Review of the Theory." *Theory into Practice*, vol. 16, no. 2:53–59.

Kohlberg, L., C. Levine, and A. Hewer. 1983. "Moral Stages: A Current Formulation and a Response to Critics." In *Contributions to Human Development, Vol. 10*. Edited by J.A. Meacham. New York: Karger.

Kurland, N.B. 1991. "The Ethical Implications of the Straight-Commission Compensation System—An Agency Perspective." *Journal of Business Ethics*, vol. 10, no. 10:757–766.

———. 1999. "Ethics and Commission." *Business and Society Review*, vol. 104, no. 1:29–33.

Lacayo, R., and A. Ripley. 2002. "Persons of the Year." *Time*, vol. 160, no. 27 (30 December):32.

Lamb, R.B. 1999. "Ethics in Financial Services." *Business and Society Review*, vol. 104, no. 1:13–17.

Lawton, Philip. 2006. "The Perfect Villain." *CFA Magazine*, vol. 17, no. 2 (March/April):6–7.

LeClair, D.T., and L. Ferrell. 2000. "Innovation in Experiential Business Ethics Training." *Journal of Business Ethics*, vol. 23, no. 3:313–322.

Leeson, N.W. 1996. *Rogue Trader: How I Brought Down Barings Bank and Shook the Financial World*. Boston: Little, Brown.

Lefcourt, H.M. 1976. *Locus of Control: Current Trends in Theory and Research*. Hillsdale, NJ: Lawrence Erlbaum.

Leitsch, D.L. 2004. "Differences in the Perceptions of Moral Intensity in the Moral Decision Process: An Empirical Examination of Accounting Students." *Journal of Business Ethics*, vol. 53, no. 3:313–323.

Lewis, M. 1989. *Liar's Poker*. New York: Norton.

Lii, P. 2001. "The Impact of Personal Gains on Cognitive Dissonance for Business Ethics Judgments." *Teaching Business Ethics*, vol. 5, no. 1:21–33.

Loe, T.W., L. Ferrell, and P. Mansfield. 2000. "A Review of Empirical Studies Assessing Ethical Decision Making in Business." *Journal of Business Ethics*, vol. 25, no. 3:185–204.

"'Lone Voice': Excerpts from Testimony of Executive Who Challenged Enron." 2002. *New York Times* (15 February):C7.

Lux, H. 1998. "The Rise and Fall of Michael Smirlock." *Institutional Investor*, vol. 32, no. 12:58.

MacIntyre, A. 1999. *Dependent Rational Animals: Why Human Beings Need the Virtues*. Chicago: Open Court.

Maclagan, P. 1998. *Management and Morality: A Developmental Perspective*. London: Sage.

Maital, S. 1982. *Minds, Markets, and Money: Psychological Foundations of Economic Behavior*. New York: Basic Books.

Martens, L.T., and K. Day. 1999. "Five Common Mistakes in Designing and Implementing a Business Ethics Program." *Business and Society Review*, vol. 104, no. 2:163–170.

McDonald, G. 2000. "Business Ethics: Practical Proposals for Organisations." *Journal of Business Ethics*, vol. 25, no. 2:169–184.

McWilliams, V., and A. Nahavandi. 2006. "Using Live Cases to Teach Ethics." *Journal of Business Ethics*, vol. 67, no. 4:421–433.

Mesmer-Magnus, J.R., and C. Viswesvaran. 2005. "Whistleblowing in Organizations: An Examination of Correlates of Whistleblowing Intentions, Actions, and Retaliation." *Journal of Business Ethics*, vol. 62, no. 3:277–297.

Messick, D.M. 1993. "Equality as a Decision Heuristic." In *Psychological Perspectives on Justice: Theory and Applications*. Edited by B. A. Mellers and J. Baron. New York: Cambridge University Press.

Messick, D.M., and M.H. Bazerman. 2001. "Ethical Leadership and the Psychology of Decision-Making." In *The Next Phase of Business Ethics: Integrating Psychology and Ethics*. Edited by J. Dienhart, D. Moberg, and R. Duska. Oxford, U.K.: Elsevier Science/JAI Press.

Milgram, S. 1963. "Behavioral Study of Obedience." *Journal of Abnormal and Social Psychology*, vol. 67, no. 4:371–378.

———.1964. "Group Pressure and Action Against a Person." *Journal of Abnormal and Social Psychology*, vol. 69, no. 2:137–143.

———. 1974. *Obedience to Authority*. New York: Harper and Row.

Miller, D.T. 2001. "The Norm of Self-Interest." In *The Next Phase of Business Ethics: Integrating Psychology and Ethics.* Edited by J. Dienhart, D. Moberg, and R. Duska. Oxford, U.K.: Elsevier Science/JAI Press.

Morgan, R.B. 1993. "Self- and Co-Worker Perceptions of Ethics and Their Relationships to Leadership and Salary." *Academy of Management Journal*, vol. 36, no. 1:200–214.

Morris, S.A., and R.A. McDonald. 1995. "The Role of Moral Intensity in Moral Judgments: An Empirical Investigation." *Journal of Business Ethics*, vol. 14, no. 9:715–726.

Moscovici, S. 1985. "Social Influence and Conformity." In *Handbook of Social Psychology*. Edited by G. Lindzey and E. Aronson. New York: Random House.

Moscovici, S., and M. Zavalloni. 1969. "The Group as a Polarizer of Attitudes." *Journal of Personality and Social Psychology*, vol. 12, no. 2:125–135.

Mudrack, P.E. 2003. "The Untapped Relevance of Moral Development Theory in the Study of Business Ethics." *Journal of Business Ethics*, vol. 42, no. 3:225–236.

Murk, D.A., and J.A. Addleman. 1992. "Relations among Moral Reasoning, Locus of Control, and Demographic Variables among College Students." *Psychological Reports*, vol. 70, no. 2:467–476.

Near, J.P., and M.P. Miceli. 1996. "Whistle-Blowing: Myth and Reality." *Journal of Management*, vol. 22, no. 3:507–526.

Nemeth, C.J. 1986. "Differential Contributions of Majority and Minority Influence." *Psychological Review*, vol. 93, no. 1:23–32.

Newcomb, T.M. 1972. "Expectations as a Social-Psychological Concept." In *Human Behavior in Economic Affairs*. Edited by B. Strumpel, J.N. Morgan, and E. Zahn. Amsterdam: Elsevier Scientific Publishing Company.

Newsome, J.P. 2005. "Ethical Issues Facing Stock Analysts." *Geneva Papers on Risk and Insurance*, vol. 30, no. 3:451–466.

Nixon, R. 1990. "I Could See No Reason to Live." *Time*, vol. 135, no. 14:34–41.

Oberlechner, T. 2004a. "Perceptions of Successful Traders by Foreign Exchange Professionals." *Journal of Behavioral Finance*, vol. 5, no. 1:23–31.

———. 2004b. *The Psychology of the Foreign Exchange Market*. Chichester, U.K.: John Wiley.

O'Fallon, M.J., and K.D. Butterfield. 2005. "A Review of the Empirical Ethical Decision-Making Literature: 1996–2003." *Journal of Business Ethics*, vol. 59, no. 4: 375–413.

Oppel, R.A. 2002. "Wall St. Analysts Faulted on Enron." *New York Times* (28 February):A1.

Osofsky, M.J., A. Bandura, and P.G. Zimbardo. 2005. "The Role of Moral Disengagement in the Execution Process." *Law and Human Behavior*, vol. 29, no. 4:371.

Pajo, K., and P. McGhee. 2003. "The Institutionalisation of Business Ethics: Are New Zealand Organisations Doing Enough?" *Journal of the Australian and New Zealand Academy of Management*, vol. 9, no. 1:52–65.

Paolillo, J.G.P., and S.J. Vitell. 2002. "An Empirical Investigation of the Influence of Selected Personal, Organizational, and Moral Intensity Factors on Ethical Decision Making." *Journal of Business Ethics*, vol. 35, no. 1:65–74.

Pardales, M.J. 2002. "'So, How Did You Arrive at That Decision?' Connecting Moral Imagination and Moral Judgment." *Journal of Moral Education*, vol. 31, no. 4:423–437.

Partnoy, F. 1997. *F.I.A.S.C.O.: Blood in the Water on Wall Street*. New York: Norton.

Pasha, S. 2006. "Enron Founder Ken Lay Dies" (http://money.cnn.com/2006/07/05/news/newsmakers/lay_death/index.htm?cnn=yes; retrieved 22 February 2007).

Pasha, S., and J. Seid. 2006. "Lay and Skilling's Day of Reckoning" (http://money.cnn.com/2006/05/25/news/newsmakers/enron_verdict/index.htm; retrieved 22 February 2007).

Payne, S.L., and R.A. Giacalone. 1990. "Social Psychological Approaches to the Perception of Ethical Dilemmas." *Human Relations*, vol. 43, no. 7:649–665.

Peterson, R.S. 2001. "Toward a More Deontological Approach to the Ethical Use of Social Influence." In *Social Influences on Ethical Behavior in Organizations*. Edited by J.M. Darley and D.M. Messick. Mahwah, NJ: Lawrence Erlbaum Associates.

Petry, E.S., A.E. Mujica, and D.M. Vickery. 1998. "Sources and Consequences of Workplace Pressure: Increasing the Risk of Unethical and Illegal Business Practices." *Business and Society Review*, vol. 99, no. 1:25–30.

Plous, S. 1993. *The Psychology of Judgment and Decision-Making*. New York: McGraw-Hill.

Ponemon, L. 1993. "The Influence of Ethical Reasoning on Auditors' Perception of Management's Integrity and Competence." *Advances in Accounting*, vol. 11:1–23.

Ponemon, L., and A. Felo. 1996. "Key Features of an Effective Ethics Training Program." *Management Accounting*, vol. 78, no. 4:66–67.

Pritchard, M.S. 1992. "Good Works." *Professional Ethics*, vol. 1, nos. 1–2:158–178.

Rest, J. 1986. *Moral Development: Advances in Research and Theory*. New York: Praeger.

Rest, J., E. Turiel, and L. Kohlberg. 1994. "Level of Moral Development as a Determinant of Preference and Comprehension of Moral Judgments Made by Others." In *Fundamental Research in Moral Development*. Edited by B. Puka. New York: Garland Publishing.

Reynolds, S.J. 2006. "Moral Awareness and Ethical Predispositions: Investigating the Role of Individual Differences in the Recognition of Moral Issues." *Journal of Applied Psychology*, vol. 91, no. 1:233–243.

Ritter, B.A. 2006. "Can Business Ethics Be Trained? A Study of the Ethical Decision-Making Process in Business Students." *Journal of Business Ethics*, vol. 68, no. 2:153–164.

Rolfe, J., and P. Troob. 2000. *Monkey Business: Swinging through the Wall Street Jungle*. New York: Warner Books.

Ross, L., and C. Anderson. 1982. "Shortcomings in the Attribution Process: On the Origins and Maintenance of Erroneous Social Assessments." In *Judgment under Uncertainty: Heuristics and Biases*. Edited by D. Kahneman, P. Slovic, and A. Tversky. New York: Cambridge University Press.

Ross, M., and D. DiTecco. 1975. "An Attributional Analysis of Moral Judgments." *Journal of Social Issues*, vol. 31, no. 3:91–109.

Rotter, J.B. 1966. "Generalized Expectancies for Internal versus External Control of Reinforcement." *Psychological Monographs: General and Applied*, vol. 80, no. 1:1–28.

Saari, L.M., T.R. Johnson, S.D. McLaughlin, and D.M. Zimmerle. 1988. "A Survey of Management Training and Education Practices in U.S. Companies." *Personnel Psychology*, vol. 41, no. 4:731–743.

Schlenker, B. 1980. *Impression Management*. New York: Brooks/Cole.

Schwartz, M.S. 2004. "Effective Corporate Codes of Ethics: Perceptions of Code Users." *Journal of Business Ethics*, vol. 55, no. 4:321–343.

SEC. 2006. "Investor Complaints and Questions." U.S. Securities and Exchange Commission (http://www.sec.gov/news/data.htm; retrieved 25 February 2007).

Selman, R.L. 1976. "Social-Cognitive Understanding: A Guide to Educational and Clinical Practice." In *Moral Development and Behavior*. Edited by T. Lickona. New York: Holt, Rinehart and Winston.

Shafer, W.E., R.E. Morris, and A.A. Ketchand. 2001. "Effects of Personal Values on Auditors' Ethical Decisions." *Accounting, Auditing & Accountability Journal*, vol. 14, no. 3:254–277.

Sherif, M. 1936. *The Psychology of Social Norms*. New York: Harper.

Simon, R. 2004. "Independent Stock Research Gets a Boost from New Study; Investment Banks' Picks Fared Worse over Time, Study Says; How to Get a Second Opinion." *Wall Street Journal* (3 August):D1.

Sims, R.L., and A.E. Gegez. 2004. "Attitudes Towards Business Ethics: A Five Nation Comparative Study." *Journal of Business Ethics*, vol. 50, no. 3:253–265.

Sims, R.L., and J.P. Keenan. 1998. "Predictors of External Whistleblowing: Organizational and Intrapersonal Variables." *Journal of Business Ethics*, vol. 17, no. 4:411–421.

Sims, R.R. 1991. "The Institutionalization of Organizational Ethics." *Journal of Business Ethics*, vol. 10, no. 7:493–506.

———. 1992. "Linking Groupthink to Unethical Behavior in Organizations." *Journal of Business Ethics*, vol. 11, no. 9:651–662.

———. 2000. "Changing an Organization's Culture under New Leadership." *Journal of Business Ethics*, vol. 25, no. 1:65–78.

Sims, R.R., and J. Brinkman. 2002. "Leaders As Moral Role Models: The Case of John Gutfreund at Salomon Brothers." *Journal of Business Ethics*, vol. 35, no. 4: 327–339.

Sims, R.R., and E.L. Felton, Jr. 2006. "Designing and Delivering Business Ethics Teaching and Learning." *Journal of Business Ethics*, vol. 63, no. 3:297–312.

Slovic, P. 1990. "Choice." In *An Invitation to Cognitive Science—Thinking*. Edited by D.N. Osherson and E.E. Smith. Cambridge, MA: MIT Press.

Smith, A. 1904. *An Inquiry into the Nature and Causes of the Wealth of Nations*. 5th ed. London: Methuen (first published in 1776).

Solomon, R.C. 1999. *A Better Way to Think about Business: How Personal Integrity Leads to Corporate Success.* New York: Oxford University Press.

Starmer, C. 1993. "The Psychology of Uncertainty in Economic Theory: A Critical Appraisal and a Fresh Approach." *Review of Political Economy*, vol. 5, no. 2:181–196.

Stevens, B. 2004. "The Ethics of the U.S. Business Executive: A Study of Perceptions." *Journal of Business Ethics*, vol. 54, no. 2:163–171.

Stewart, J.B. 1991. *Den of Thieves.* New York: Simon & Schuster.

Stoner, J.A. 1961. *A Comparison of Individual and Group Decisions Involving Risk.* Cambridge, MA: MIT Press.

Strudler, A., and D.E. Warren. 2001. "Authority, Heuristics, and the Structure of Excuses." In *Social Influences on Ethical Behavior in Organizations.* Edited by J.M. Darley and D.M. Messick. Mahwah, NJ: Lawrence Erlbaum Associates.

Sweeney, J.T., and R.W. Roberts. 1997. "Cognitive Moral Development and Auditor Independence." *Accounting, Organizations and Society*, vol. 22, nos. 3–4: 337–352.

Tavakoli, A.A., J.P. Keenan, and B. Cranjak-Karanovic. 2003. "Culture and Whistleblowing: An Empirical Study of Croatian and United States Managers Utilizing Hofstede's Cultural Dimensions." *Journal of Business Ethics*, vol. 43, nos. 1–2:49–64.

Trevino, L.K. 1986. "Ethical Decision Making in Organizations: A Person-Situation Interactionist Model." *Academy of Management Review*, vol. 11, no. 3: 601–617.

Trevino, L.K., and G.A. Ball. 1992. "The Social Implications of Punishing Unethical Behavior: Observers' Cognitive and Affective Reactions." *Journal of Management*, vol. 18, no. 4:751–768.

Trevino, L.K., and K.A. Nelson. 2007. *Managing Business Ethics: Straight Talk about How to Do It Right.* 4th ed. Hoboken, NJ: Wiley.

Trevino, L.K., and S.A. Youngblood. 1990. "Bad Apples in Bad Barrels: A Causal Analysis of Ethical Decision-Making Behavior." *Journal of Applied Psychology*, vol. 75, no. 4:378–385.

Trevino, L.K., K.D. Butterfield, and D.L. McCabe. 1995. "Contextual Influences on Ethics-Related Outcomes in Organizations: Rethinking Ethical Climate and Ethical Culture." Unpublished paper presented at the Annual Academy of Management Meeting.

Tversky, A., and D. Kahneman. 1973. "Availability: A Heuristic for Judging Frequency and Probability." *Cognitive Psychology*, vol. 5, no. 2:207–232.

———. 1974. "Judgment under Uncertainty: Heuristics and Biases." *Science*, vol. 185, no. 4157:1124–1131.

Tyson, T. 1990. "Believing That Everyone Else Is Less Ethical: Implications for Work Behavior and Ethics Instruction." *Journal of Business Ethics*, vol. 9, no. 9: 715–721.

Valentine, S., and T. Barnett. 2002. "Ethics Codes and Sales Professionals' Perceptions of Their Organizations' Ethical Values." *Journal of Business Ethics*, vol. 40, no. 3:191–200.

Valentine, S., and A. Johnson. 2005. "Codes of Ethics, Orientation Programs, and the Perceived Importance of Employee Incorruptibility." *Journal of Business Ethics*, vol. 61, no. 1:45–53.

Valentine, S., and G. Fleischman. 2004. "Ethics Training and Businesspersons' Perceptions of Organizational Ethics." *Journal of Business Ethics*, vol. 52, no. 4:391–400.

Valentine, S., L. Godkin, and M. Lucero. 2002. "Ethical Context, Organizational Commitment, and Person-Organization Fit." *Journal of Business Ethics*, vol. 41, no. 4:349–360.

VanSandt, C., J. Shepard, and S. Zappe. 2006. "An Examination of the Relationship between Ethical Work Climate and Moral Awareness." *Journal of Business Ethics*, vol. 68, no. 4:409–432.

Veit, E.T., and M.R. Murphy. 1996. "Ethics Violations: A Survey of Investment Analysts." *Journal of Business Ethics*, vol. 15, no. 12:1287–1297.

Velasquez, M.G., and C. Rostankowski. 1985. *Ethics: Theory and Practice*. Englewood Cliffs, NJ: Prentice-Hall.

Verschoor, C.C. 2006. "Strong Ethics Is a Critical Quality of Leadership." *Strategic Finance*, vol. 87, no. 7:19–20.

Vidaver-Cohen, D. 1998. "Moral Imagination in Organizational Problem-Solving: An Institutional Perspective." *Business Ethics Quarterly*, Special Issue No. 1:123–148.

———. 2001. "Motivational Appeal in Normative Theories of Enterprise." In *The Next Phase of Business Ethics: Integrating Psychology and Ethics*. Edited by J. Dienhart, D. Moberg, and R. Duska. Oxford, U.K.: Elsevier Science/JAI Press.

Weirich, T.R., and R.W. Rouse. 2003. "Sarbanes–Oxley Bill: New Challenges for the Financial Professional." *Journal of Corporate Accounting and Finance*, vol. 14, no. 2:55–61.

Welles, C. 1988. "What Led Beech-Nut Down the Road to Disgrace." *Business Week* (22 February):124–128.

Werhane, P.H. 1998. "Moral Imagination and the Search for Ethical Decision-Making in Management." *Business Ethics Quarterly*, Special Issue No. 1:75–98.

Williams, O.F. 1998. *The Moral Imagination: How Literature and Films Can Stimulate Ethical Reflection in the Business World.* Notre Dame, IN: University of Notre Dame Press.

Wolf, S. 1985. "Manifest and Latent Influence of Majorities and Minorities." *Journal of Personality and Social Psychology*, vol. 48:899–908.

Zajonc, R.B. 2000. "Feeling and Thinking: Closing the Debate over the Independence of Affect." In *Feeling and Thinking: The Role of Affect in Social Cognition*. Edited by J.P. Forgas. Cambridge, U.K.: Cambridge University Press.

Zajonc, R.B., and H. Markus. 1982. "Affective and Cognitive Factors in Preferences." *Journal of Consumer Research*, vol. 9, no. 2:123–131.

Zeckhauser, R., J. Patel, and D. Hendricks. 1991. "Nonrational Actors and Financial Market Behavior." *Theory and Decision*, vol. 31, nos. 2–3:257–287.

Zimbardo, P.G. 1976. "Making Sense of Senseless Vandalism." In *Current Perspectives in Social Psychology*. 4th ed. Edited by E.P. Hollander and R.G. Hunt. Oxford, U.K.: Oxford University Press.

———. 1982. "Pathology of Imprisonment." In *Readings in Social Psychology: Contemporary Perspectives*. Edited by D. Krebs. New York: Harper and Row.

———. 1995. "The Psychology of Evil: A Situationist Perspective on Recruiting Good People to Engage in Anti-Social Acts." *Japanese Journal of Social Psychology*, vol. 11, no. 2:125–133.

———. 2004. "A Situationist Perspective on the Psychology of Evil: Understanding How Good People Are Transformed into Perpetrators." In *Social Psychology of Good and Evil*. Edited by A.G. Miller. New York: Guilford Press.

———. 2007. *The Lucifer Effect: Understanding How Good People Turn Evil.* New York: Random House.